WIDOW IN THE CITY

WIDOW IN THE CITY

A Memoir of Heartbreaks and Hookups

AMY GABRIELLE

SHE WRITES PRESS

Published in 2026 by
She Writes Press, an imprint of The Stable Book Group

1569 Solano Ave #546
Berkeley, CA 94707
https://shewritespress.com

Library of Congress Control Number: 2026900599

ISBN: 979-8-89636-200-5
eISBN: 979-8-89636-201-2

Interior Designer: Andrea Reider

Printed in the United States

Names and identifying characteristics have been changed to protect the privacy of certain individuals. Events, locales and conversations are recollected to the best of the author's memory.

For Steven Harris

PROLOGUE

February 2022

I WAS SURPRISED by how tall Eli was. I'm five foot two inches, and he had to be at least a foot taller. He'd probably put this asset on his dating profile, but I never paid attention to that stuff. A man's height is not that important to me.

I invited him inside and we sat down on the couch. We spent fifteen minutes talking about his work: Bitcoin and Ethereum, art, and NFTs (non-fungible tokens). All the while he was running his hand up and down my leg.

Eli had been working from home that morning, so he was dressed casually in jeans and a sweater. I was comfortable in my pink crotchless panties underneath black yoga pants. I had them slung high on my hips, so they peeked out over the top of my waistband. On top I was wearing a tight T-shirt and no bra, my nipples visibly hard against the chill in the apartment.

He asked if he could have a tour, but we both knew it was a pretense. I assumed we'd stop in my bedroom, but Eli let me lead him into the master bathroom, where I braced myself facing the sink. He stood behind me, rubbing my breasts, and I could feel the condensation from his hot breath against my cool neck.

He plunged his hand down the front of my pants, stroking the soft skin between my legs as I moved my hips back and forth. He paused before he spun me around and lifted me up onto the vanity. Jars of creams and lotions clattered to the ground as we hastily discarded the rest of our clothes, and he put on a condom.

I wrapped my legs around his waist, pulling him closer as he slid inside me. My body was fully engaged in the present moment, but my mind wandered back in time.

A year ago, my husband and I had celebrated our son's ninth birthday as a happy family of three. Six months ago, he'd prepared his special homemade lasagna for our thirteenth wedding anniversary. Three months ago, I joined Bumble. A month ago, I joined Feeld, a kink-friendly dating app. Two weeks ago, I sent naked photos of myself to a man with whom I'd just matched. Last week, I secretly sexted while out to lunch with my colleagues, and now here I was in the middle of the afternoon having sex with a stranger in my bathroom.

How did everything change so drastically and so quickly?

"Incurable cancer," the doctors said. "Three to five years."

We were hoping for five.

We only got three.

As Eli's thrusts gained momentum, I reflected on what I was doing and who I was becoming.

Was I going crazy, or was this some weird manifestation of grief?

He wasn't even my first lover since Steven died; he was actually my third. I wondered if it even mattered.

For some reason, as I moved into this new life as a widow it felt important to me to keep a historically accurate record of what I did and with whom. After each encounter I'd write down their names and dates in a small Moleskine notebook I kept in the top drawer of my bedside table; maybe I would have trusted myself to remember those details if I'd had more orgasms. But it took time for me to develop the level of trust I needed to climax with a new partner. In the months since my husband had passed away, I had become successful at attracting men, but my fear of being left again also made me an expert at pushing them away.

I'll write his name down later, I thought to myself.

I squeezed my legs tighter around Eli's waist, hoping this would encourage him to finish up soon. I only had an hour before I had to pick up my son from school.

At that moment, what I wanted more than anything was to drop back into my body and get out of my head. Lately I had trouble concentrating on anything for very long. Collecting information wasn't the problem, but retaining it took extra effort, even when it was just the latest guy I spent time with.

Saving texts and jotting down details such as names, dates, and places were convenient souvenirs, evidence of what had happened during this chaotic period in my life. Still, I missed the days when I had the mental clarity to write down my thoughts and feelings in a diary. I accepted that at this moment, digital documentation was more accessible to me than keeping a traditional written record given my extended bout of brain fog (menopause? grief?). Hopefully, that would clear up sooner rather than later. In the meantime, I was relying on technology.

At least purchasing more space in "the cloud" was inexpensive, and since my husband's death I really did need that space. Since he'd died, I had developed a mini obsession with lingerie and sexy costumes and taken hundreds of photos of myself in various stages of undress (including complete). I'd always just worn cotton underwear when Steven was alive, I'd felt confident in my own skin and in my marriage. When he died, sexy costumes and lingerie made me feel desirable and wanted again. Curating a new collection of sensual garments kept me distracted from the magnitude of my loss, while my photoshoots got me out of bed and into the shower on a regular basis.

As I redirected my attention back to Eli I wondered if I would see him again. I sort of wanted to, but not enough to care too much if I didn't. My past relationships had either been very long-term and heterosexually monogamous or one-time hookups. Could Eli and I sustain something ongoing and casual, or would he disappear like the first two guys?

CHAPTER ONE

FINALLY! Why did it take so long for a tween boy to fall asleep? The hum of the air conditioner had almost lulled me to sleep first. Henry slept under a heavy blanket, so we kept the room cold even though the nights had already become cooler by the end of September.

I tried to imagine the day my son wouldn't want me to stay in his room until I was sure he was unconscious, but I couldn't. Henry never wanted to be alone. He never played by himself in his room and couldn't fall asleep without one of his parents present. When Steven was alive, we'd taken turns sitting in the tan leather club chair stationed in the corner of his bedroom.

Fuck, I had always hated that chair. It had the distinction, in my eyes, of being both ugly and uncomfortable. To Steven, it was the first piece of "real" furniture he bought when he moved back to New York after business school. I knew what it meant to be a little sentimental about furniture; I still had a set of drawers from Pottery Barn in my closet that I had bought over twenty-five years ago. When we moved in together, I'd hoped he would sell or give the club chair away, but it was the one thing he wasn't willing to compromise on. So ultimately, I caved. I had already vetoed the three-foot-tall Cartman doll a friend had given him, along with a third of his extensive T-shirt collection. I hadn't watched *South Park*, but even if I had, I wasn't going to waste precious square footage on something that served no practical purpose. Since Steven died, I'd had to sit in that chair every single night, and it was exhausting.

When I was sure Henry was asleep, I tiptoed out and walked toward the kitchen. Halfway there I thought I heard a noise so I froze mid step, fearful that Henry would call me back to his room. I could usually tell when it was safe to get up and go, but occasionally he would still be on the edge of consciousness. If he opened his eyes and realized I was gone, he'd call out in an ever-increasing monotone, "Mom. Mom. *Mom!!!!*" until I sat back down in the chair for another twenty to thirty minutes. I knew he was afraid to be alone, but I felt annoyed when I had to go back and sit with him again. Then I'd feel guilty for feeling annoyed with my frightened son.

I stood completely still and listened. All was quiet, and relief washed over me. I felt even more highly attuned to Henry's needs and feelings since Steven's death, and I was only free from worry, guilt, and annoyance when he was safely sleeping in his bed. Tonight, I needed that freedom.

When Steven's death certificate arrived in the mail a month after he died, his loss hit me in a whole new way. The administration of his death required that I notify multiple entities, including financial institutions and government agencies. I'd ordered ten copies.

The first order of business was submitting a claim for his life insurance policy.

I slipped my pointer finger under the flap of the thick manila envelope and pried it open. It felt surreal to be holding proof that my husband was dead, but I was also detached from the reality that I would never see Steven again. I knew he was "gone," but my brain kept telling me he must be somewhere. I could not grasp the idea that he was nowhere.

I barely remembered providing Steven's personal details to the funeral home director the night he died. I was so exhausted after that horrific day at the hospital. I should have had his required information saved in an easily accessible place, and I was mad that I hadn't been up to my usual organizational standards.

As I continued to look over the document, I noticed that something felt off about his social security number. Had I made a mistake when I'd spoken to the funeral home director? I was sure I knew his number by heart, especially after filling out all his disability paperwork and staying on top of his affairs since he'd fallen ill.

I decided to check it against his actual social security card, which was still in his wallet by the front door with his keys. As I compared the two, I noticed that the first number was supposed to be a one, instead of a zero. I felt sick as I realized all ten copies were useless.

How long would it take to get this corrected?

Google informed me that the New York City Department of Records estimated four to six weeks.

Panic rose up inside me as I thought, *I can't possibly wait that long.*

I was surprised by how vulnerable I felt after Steven died. I had always been a highly capable person, but now I worried that I wouldn't be able to care for Henry on my own. I convinced myself that I would feel safe and secure again after

I cashed in Steven's life insurance policy. I didn't technically need the money right away, but on an emotional level I felt desperate to have it.

I'd spent the last three years worried about him dying, wondering how I would live without him, and now that I had survived his death, I felt convinced that I could do almost anything.

I Googled, "Can you erase printer ink?" and found several videos that demonstrated how it could be scraped off with a razor blade.

I retrieved the X-Acto knife from the kitchen junk drawer and sat down at the large dining room table. I placed a copy of the death certificate in front of me and leaned in very close, my eyeball almost touching the paper.

Turning the blade on its side, I began gently scraping it across the misprint.

Fearful I had applied too much pressure, I held the paper up to the ceiling light. A pinprick of cool white light shined through a tiny hole.

"Fuck," I swore softly.

My rationalization for starting this whole endeavor was that I was "righting" a wrong, like any good wife would do. I wasn't even worried that I would fuck it up because I had nine copies to practice on.

It turned out not to be so easy to scrape off printer ink without cutting through the paper. At first, I didn't realize I also had to be careful not to disturb any of the watermarks. But I continued to work.

Nine mangled death certificates later I checked the time on my phone—it was 2 a.m.

Those nine certificates lay at my feet, surrounding me like kindling for a funeral pyre.

Luckily the tenth one was the charm.

Once I successfully scraped off the zero, I painstakingly measured where the replacement number should be printed. I felt almost giddy as I looked at the finished product.

Pretty damn good, but the paper under the newly printed number looked a little worn in comparison to the rest of the document's crispness.

I had been laser focused on getting the insurance money, but in that moment, I felt a sudden flash of guilt that I wasn't more bereft. Wouldn't a "normal" grieving wife have fallen apart upon seeing her husband's death certificate for the first time? Maybe she would be so devastated that she crumpled up the evidence? I was almost sure she would have cried. But it wasn't that I was abnormal. I was just afraid that if I allowed myself to start crying, I'd never stop.

I scrunched the document into a ball and then smoothed it out flat on the table. The newly formed creases did a pretty good job of masking the worn area, but it needed something more to make it blend in. I figured fake tears would do the job.

I filled a bowl with warm water, dipped my fingers in, and then flicked droplets all over the paper. The results were amazing, but would I really send it in with a claim form? Perhaps the certificate's condition warranted an explanation.

I leaned across the table, grabbed a pack of green Post-its and a pen, and scribbled, *I'm sorry for the condition of this death certificate. I've been very upset about my husband's death, and this is my only copy.*

I stuck it on the folded paper and sealed it in a number ten envelope.

I wasn't sure I had the courage to mail it in, but fixing Steven's death certificate had kept me occupied for several hours instead of ruminating on how much stuff I had to go through before Henry and I moved next week. It had been something to focus on other than the dismantling of our lives together one closet or cabinet at a time.

I felt a wave of sadness as I put the X-Acto knife back in the kitchen, the room which had always been Steven's domain. I already knew I wasn't going to bring all his special gadgets and appliances with us to the new apartment. We had plenty of room for everything, but there was no one there to use them.

I'd already gone through the contents of every kitchen drawer and cabinet, smiling when I saw we owned both a slow cooker and an Instant Pot. I almost heard Steven's voice trying to convince me that we needed both because some dishes simmered all day, while others demanded a rolling boil. *I'm sorry babe*, I thought, *I'm never going to use either*.

In the bedroom, as I pulled down a stack of his old baseball caps, a thick layer of dust came down with it.

"Fuck," I said, wiping my eyes with the hem of my shirt.

I was tired and angry that Steven had left me to do all the sorting and packing alone.

Before his death I had planned to help him go through all his stuff. He tended to hold onto things far too long.

Now I decided to get rid of almost everything in his closet. It didn't make sense to schlep all his clothes, old textbooks, and enormous diploma plaques to a place he wouldn't live. There were some smaller things I kept, like the wooden box filled with his beloved cufflink collection, and some of his silk ties. He loved the ones with tiny animals; his favorite were the dolphins. I figured Henry might want to use them when he got older. I also couldn't bring myself to get rid of everything that Steven loved.

When our apartment sale seemed imminent, we had looked at a few rentals near Henry's school, but ultimately, I ended up having to choose for us. Would Steven have approved of the one I rented? He could be very particular at times, but for the most part he let me have the deciding vote.

I would have convinced him that the new place checked all our post-pandemic boxes: It was renovated, on a low floor (no waiting for elevators), and a five-minute walk to Henry's school. I knew the rent was more than he'd have wanted to pay, but I would have reminded him that we only planned to be there a year or two.

The Junkluggers arrived on the 2nd of October, the day after the movers, to cart away most of the furniture and whatever else was left behind. Goodwill would decide what was salvageable and what would end up in a landfill.

I really debated about that fucking club chair. I didn't want to bring it with us, but I didn't want it to end up in the garbage either. I decided to ask the buyers if there were any pieces they wanted since I was leaving everything, except Henry's bed, which he insisted would come with us.

They told me they loved the club chair; that was the only thing they wanted. I felt like this was a sign from Steven, and I was doing the right thing by making sure it went to a family who appreciated it as much as he did.

CHAPTER TWO

STEVEN DIED at 6 p.m. on a Wednesday in August 2021. The lights were dimmed, and the shades were drawn against the Western sky where the sun still lingered.

Music played from my phone over the low hum of machines, like white noise just beneath the surface. Despite the air conditioning it was warm and close in the small room.

I took off my mask, which was already sodden with tears. A tissue materialized in front of me, and I snatched it. My sinuses were swollen shut; I smelled nothing.

His limp hand in mine, still warm with life, I whispered over and over, "You were the best husband and father." The words came instinctually, without forethought. Steven had to know how much he was appreciated while I tried to convince myself that Henry and I would be okay without him.

Someone asked me if I was ready, and I said yes even though I was not. The white noise stopped; the room plunged into silence. A voice broke through, "He's gone."

I'd arrived at the hospital that morning at 10 a.m. expecting to sit with Steven as the doctors weaned him off the high-flow oxygen machine and onto a portable tank so he could come home to hospice. Instead, a nurse brought me to a much smaller room on a higher floor. Steven had gone into heart failure and was already brain dead, and the high-flow oxygen machine was keeping his body alive.

The nurses tried to prepare me for his death. They told me that he wouldn't feel any discomfort or pain when the machine was turned off, but it would appear as if he was gasping for breath. They said it would be a more peaceful death for *me* if he was completely sedated.

What could I say? I didn't want the last memories I had of my husband to be him gasping for breath, and he would not want to be remembered that way. I felt duty bound to ensure his tranquil transition from this life to the next. I agreed to sedate him, which meant ordering a significant amount of morphine from the hospital pharmacy. I will never regret that decision, but I had no idea it would take all day to fill the order.

Steven's stepmother was with me most of the day. We had a good relationship, but I never shied away from a disagreement, and she avoided conflict at all costs. We found common ground in our love of travel and the arts, but that day at the hospital we didn't talk much. In truth, I was angry at her for suggesting I shouldn't tell anyone that I "pulled the plug" (her words) on Steven. I prided myself on being a badass, and in my mind, that meant making the hard decisions that others couldn't or wouldn't. I saw my choice as an act of bravery and love, and I would not allow her to paint it in any other light.

I was grateful that she had to go back to her apartment at 5 p.m. to wait for Henry. He was on his way back from Legoland, where he'd spent the day with some family friends. It just felt right that I should be alone with Steven when he died. No one else knew him or loved him like I did.

After I said goodbye to my husband for the last time, I waited in the hallway for one of the nurses to bring me his wedding ring and the contact information for the funeral home. I planned to donate his body to a local medical school, which meant that it had to be delivered to them within twenty-four hours.

In the elevator on my way down, I saw the same nurse who had brought me upstairs that morning. She cried when she saw me, but I remained dry-eyed. I had to go pick Henry up and tell him that his father was dead. I couldn't afford to break down and become too overwhelmed to take care of my son.

I thought I knew how I would react when Steven died. I imagined being grief stricken, of course, and perhaps unable to function for a short time. Then, I would start to heal slowly and get back to my old self.

But my grief was nothing like I expected.

At first, I didn't want to feel anything. I had our nine-year-old son to care for. He was both gifted and on the autism spectrum, and now he only had me to take care of him.

While giving him a bath the morning after his father died, he asked, "When am I getting a new dad?"

My heart physically hurt that he'd never feel Steven's pure love and devotion again. All I could do was tell him stories about all the time they spent together and hope it was enough for Henry to carry his daddy with him into the future. I couldn't admit to my son, or to myself, that his father was gone forever, and his love could never be replaced.

My plan was to get through the year of "firsts" without Steven (holidays, birthdays, anniversaries, etc.) and then

Henry and I could move forward with a new man in our lives. That seemed reasonable enough. So, I clumsily explained that it was just the two of us for now, but maybe one day I would find someone to marry who would love us both.

I was caught off guard by how lonely I felt not only in that moment, but as time dragged on. Steven and I had been together nearly twenty-four seven for the last eighteen months because of Covid. I worked remotely, and Steven was on disability. From March through October 2020 Henry was home with us, too, "unschooling," because distance learning proved too chaotic for him. He was already ahead in school, so why not let him spend more time with his dad? As I rinsed the shampoo from his hair, I was so grateful they had so much extra time together.

My best friend Lisa arrived from Chicago the evening after Steven died. She stayed with her mom, who had an apartment near mine in Manhattan, and came to hang out with Henry and me during the day. I was both disoriented and comforted when I first saw her. How had it only been a day since Steven died? It felt like weeks had passed.

Lisa and I spent the next few days working on Lego projects with Henry, drinking coffee, and planning Steven's Zoom memorial. Covid was still a concern in New York City, so I didn't want to do anything in person. I hadn't planned a service in advance because that would have meant I'd accepted he would die. I had always held onto an irrational belief that the doctors were wrong, and that Steven had a long life ahead of him. Either that, or I would find a miracle cure.

That's why Steven's death felt unexpected even though he had been living with incurable cancer for three years. When he was admitted to the hospital a week before his death with pneumonia, the doctors thought he would be released within a couple of days. I was furious that they realized too late that the cumulative effects of chemotherapy had caused irreparable damage to his heart.

He wanted to come home, but Steven died in the hospital. While I was relieved that I didn't have to watch him die slowly in our living room, it took me two years to release the anger I felt toward his doctors for not knowing how close to death he really was. It took me just as long to forgive myself for not being able to fulfill his final wish.

Thankfully Lisa took charge. "Email me a list of contacts and I'll help you pick a bunch of photos," she said. "I'll put together a video and send out the invitation with a Zoom link."

"I'm glad you're here," I said, slightly embarrassed.

I hadn't wanted her to come, but the minute I told her Steven had died she said she was getting on a plane. Of course she would come. We had known each other for fifty years, having met in nursery school when she was three and I was four years old.

The truth was, I just wanted to be alone and pretend like none of this was happening. I wanted to run away to a place where nobody knew me, where there were no expectations about how I should feel or act. But I couldn't break down. There was too much to do.

Four days after Steven died, family and friends gathered virtually to share memories of him, followed by a five-minute video montage. Since the service was primarily for me, I chose to listen rather than speak while Lisa ran the show.

She kept everyone on time so we could clock out after an hour. Henry played in his room rather than watch the service live, but we recorded it.

Steven's younger brother spoke first from Seattle, where he lived with his wife and eighteen-year-old daughter. While there was a lot of love between them, they were not particularly close.

My brother spoke next about all the Thanksgivings and Christmases we spent together. When Steven moved in with me, just six months after we met, my brother was living in the building next door with his wife and two children. We did a good amount of babysitting for them before they moved to a nearby suburb when the kids were eight and twelve years old.

My niece, now a twenty-one-year-old college graduate, was in tears. "I remember all the fun sleepovers, McDonald's for dinner, and Uncle Steven's homemade ice cream."

That was the only time I felt a little emotional as I watched in gallery view, my tiny square anchored in the upper left-hand corner of the screen. I loved my niece as if she was my first baby; seeing her hurting tore at my heart.

There were very few relatives from older generations. My father was the only parent still alive, but he was too frail to participate after a year of Covid isolation. My brother and I were still in the process of getting him into an assisted living facility. Both of Steven's parents were dead. His dad had passed the year before, and his mom had died from ovarian cancer when he was a senior in high school.

Steven's stepmother was there, and she shared some sweet stories from his twenties and thirties. His aunt (mother's sister) and a couple of first cousins shared memories from his childhood.

That was pretty much all the family we had. My mother had been estranged from her parents and siblings when she died two and a half years earlier, and my father's only sister had died at the end of April 2021.

There were still about sixty people on the call as Steven was loved by so many; old friends, parents from our babysitting co-op, and colleagues from past jobs all spoke of his kindness and generosity. The one thing I heard over and over was how devoted Steven was to Henry and me. I knew he loved us, of course I knew, but the last year and a half had been especially difficult. Hearing about the impact he'd had on others made me feel grateful for the time that we had together and also even more hurt and angry about his death.

When the pandemic descended on New York City in March 2020, I immediately wanted to rent a house near my brother in Larchmont, NY, because Steven's immune system was so compromised. We were seeing stories on the news about trailers being converted into makeshift morgues in hospital parking lots because there wasn't enough room for all the bodies. I couldn't imagine what would happen if Steven needed to be hospitalized. I refused to let myself think about him dying without me by his side.

I also felt trapped inside our two-bedroom, one-bathroom apartment. It was miserable working remotely from our bedroom while in the living room Steven attempted to supervise Henry in his second grade Google classroom. It didn't go well, and I was angry that both resisted leaving. Even though they didn't want to move, by April 1st, 2020, we were settled into an Airbnb a few blocks away from where my brother lived with his family. We kept pretty much to ourselves, but there was plenty of room to spread out. I was relieved we had escaped the chaos of the city, and Henry and Steven slowly adjusted to our temporary home. Being near my brother had kept me sane, and even though this service was painful, it was also a reminder of how many people had cared about our family.

The service ended and I was so grateful to Lisa for having pulled it off. I never could have gotten through it without her. That kind of friendship is priceless.

"I can't believe you're only here for two more days," I was close to whining as Lisa prepared to return to her life in Chicago.

She had been in the city for almost two weeks. I knew she needed to get home, but I didn't know how I was going to do this parenting thing alone.

"I know," she said, "but I can pick Henry up from school tomorrow if that helps."

"Yes, that would be great! You guys can just take a cab back here."

"That's going to get expensive. Any update about the apartment sale?"

We'd been reluctant to sell the only home we'd shared together, but neither Henry, Steven, nor I could handle the additional stress of the public school's chaotic post-pandemic environment. During that time, all three of us needed a higher level of support, the type only available in a costly private school for children with special needs.

"We're closing November sixteenth, but I want to move by the beginning of October. I'm going to see three rentals on Friday while Henry is in school."

"Oh, I wish I could stay and help you pack!"

"It's fine. I'm in get-shit-done mode."

I didn't realize at the time that "get-shit-done mode" meant avoiding the *real* shit of dealing with my grief over losing my husband and the life we shared together. Somehow, I thought if I stayed focused on tasks, I could move forward with my life rather than remain devastated by Steven's death. I gave Lisa a huge hug, so grateful to have a friend like her in my life for so many years. She never attempted to rescue me or challenge my ability to get shit done, but she knew when I needed her and how best to support me—even when I had no idea about what I needed or wanted.

CHAPTER THREE

I FELT A SENSE of relief when we moved the first week of October because it meant I could easily walk Henry to and from school. Although I knew he was safe with his teachers and therapists, it also gave me peace of mind to know I could get to him quickly if he needed me.

Everything about my life felt like it had changed, and I no longer fit into the old one. I had lived on the sixteenth floor in our post-war apartment complex, with sweeping views of the Hudson River, for seventeen years.

Now Henry and I lived on the street level of a townhouse that was built at the turn of the twentieth century. We had only moved three miles south of our old neighborhood, but it felt like another world. To be honest, I was happy to get away from everyone who knew me. I felt the need to isolate, and I especially liked that I could come and go without running into anyone in an elevator or lobby.

Our old building was filled with parents and children, and Steven and I had a large circle of friends. We did almost all our socializing as a family. When he died, I felt like an outsider, the only single parent whose life was changed forever while everyone else went on as if nothing had happened. I felt isolated and angry. Why couldn't it have been someone else's husband who got terminal cancer?

The upper floors of our new building had been divided into studio and one-bedroom apartments, occupied by single people and young couples. I didn't care that Henry was the only child living in the building, I wanted to focus on creating a new life for just the two of us first.

Our new three-bedroom, two-bathroom residence spanned the whole first floor, and was the only part of the town-house which had been completely renovated. An abundance of recessed lighting and designer ceiling fixtures had been installed to make up for the lack of direct sunlight and the entire place was climate controlled by central air conditioning.

A massive kitchen island, ten feet by four feet, dominated the open floor plan at the back of the apartment. Next to the front door was a small guest bathroom, and off the long hall-way were two small rooms, my office and Henry's bedroom. At the front, facing the street, was the master suite with a custom tiled bathroom, including a rain shower and freestanding soak-ing tub. I absolutely loved it; it felt like a dream come true.

Although living close to Henry's school made my life eas-ier in some ways, it felt painful going to events there by myself. I stuck out as the only single parent, and I felt the full weight of Steven's absence. It wasn't until the school's Halloween car-nival that I remembered how much he loved getting into cos-tume when Henry was little. One year they went as the Man in the Yellow Hat and Curious George. They were too cute, but I didn't have it in me to play that role for Henry—and I avoided school events whenever possible.

Being around people was exhausting, and I had become incapable of small talk. I dreaded the impending holidays and going back to work in December, but nighttime was the worst. It had been long before Steven died when I began sleeping on the couch a couple of nights a week. He was never a deep sleeper, but the effects of chemo made him very restless.

The first time he kicked me I was so startled; I had no idea what had happened. When he did it again, I felt utterly rejected, like he was subconsciously kicking me out of our bed. I felt unlovable and unworthy to sleep next to him. I never said anything because I knew he wasn't doing it intentionally, but it still hurt.

A few months before Steven died, I woke him up because I was having a terrible panic attack. He held me in bed as I cried a river of tears onto his T-shirt. It was one of the few times I let him see me scared. I begged him not to leave me. He said he didn't want to, and that he was doing everything he could to stay. I knew that was the truth, but I wanted him to promise he wouldn't die.

Now that he was gone, the combination of darkness and loneliness felt like they would swallow me whole. My short-term disability was approved with a note from my psychiatrist. I didn't feel depressed, not in the clinical sense, but I was unable to return to work.

I was all too familiar with clinical depression, having been diagnosed with anxiety and depression when I was nineteen years old, more than half my lifetime ago. While Steven's death was undoubtedly the largest loss I had ever suffered, because of my responsibilities with Henry I didn't want to stay in bed all day. There was also so much unpacking to do, and I wanted us settled.

My brother came into the city for a visit on the first day of November. He wanted to see the new apartment and check on how we were doing. He arrived early, while Henry was still in school, so we'd have some time to talk alone.

He was worried because I had distanced myself from most of my friends, and he thought I was spending too much time alone. I felt my isolation was a way of taking care of myself, but when he recommended I sign up for Bumble or Tinder, I wasn't opposed to the idea.

"You can go on a few dates and get out of the apartment," he said.

The truth was, I had already started to think about other men. I was lonely, and still angry at Steven for leaving me, whether that made sense or not. I'd spent the last three years wondering how I would live without him, how I would raise Henry alone. Now that I had survived his death, I felt panicked, but also emboldened, to do whatever I wanted. I was still alive, without the specter of death hanging over my head. For some people it may have seemed too soon to start dating, but after everything I had been through it felt right for me.

"Okay, I'll try Bumble first," I said, handing him my phone. "Just take a couple of photos for my profile. All my recent pictures include Steven and Henry."

It took me a while to figure out the Bumble app. I preferred working on my laptop rather than my phone, but some of the functionality was lost in the browser. At least my Samsung had a large screen. We'd always had Androids instead of iPhones because Steven felt that Apple's cybersecurity had too many holes in it. He was a data architect, so I thought he knew best. I still hadn't canceled his phone or taken him off the account as the manager of our Verizon family plan, but now I thought maybe it was time.

The irony wasn't lost on me that three years ago I was furious with him when I broke my phone and couldn't get a new one without his access codes. He'd been in the hospital recovering from the surgery that excised his tumor, and I was completely stressed out because it was the first time I was looking after Henry by myself.

I had felt so scared about the future. How would I care for Henry without Steven? I couldn't even replace my fucking cell phone. Frustrated, I stormed into Steven's hospital room, feeling like a 1950s housewife who needed her husband's permission to replace her phone.

"Why are you the account manager?" I demanded.

Rather than answer my question he asked what happened to my old phone.

"I was frustrated and threw it on the ground," I said.

He thought I had a protective cover on it.

"I did," I hissed, "but then I stomped on it for good measure."

It was easier for me to get angry than admit that I felt helpless and scared. It made me feel powerful rather than vulnerable. I was so mad I even asked one of the social workers if they could send my husband to rehab rather than home at the end of the week. They told me he would heal faster at home, so I let it go, but I was still fuming.

Now that I was experiencing all the grief and pain of having lost Steven, along with the huge responsibility of being a mom on my own, I was also becoming aware that there was a level of freedom and choice I now had, including the freedom to make different choices about things like furniture or cell phones. Including the freedom to date.

It took me a while to find some photos of myself without either Steven or Henry in the frame. I realized that these new dating apps were different from the pre-smartphone, web-based ones I had used over ten years ago. They relied more heavily on photos and were shorter on biographic information.

Soon after I finished my profile I matched with Jay. Women had to make the first move on Bumble, but I had no idea what to write in the chat.

Steven and I had never been big texters. We preferred to hear each other's voices during the day. God, I missed that. I felt awkward and scared to reach out to Jay, like somehow, he could see me through the phone. I told myself that this wasn't a big deal, I didn't have to commit to anything.

I typed, "Hey, how's your day going?"

He responded right away, "I'm good, what are you up to?"

Jay didn't live in my neighborhood, but he worked nearby.

"Let's have lunch next week. Do you like Mexican food?" he asked.

"Yes, I love Mexican food!"

Ugh, why did I use an exclamation point? Henry would have said, "That's so cringe, Mom." But I was so out of practice. I hadn't been on a date in fourteen years. I had no idea what to expect, or even what I wanted.

CHAPTER FOUR

NEW YORK CITY was in a cold snap the first half of November, and temperatures remained below freezing. I wasn't looking forward to facing the frigid weather, but hopefully my date with Jay would be worth it.

It took me longer than expected to decide what to wear. Ultimately, I settled on an oversized gray sweater and black jeans under my full-length Canada Goose puffer. Steven would have balked at the price of the puffer, but I'd made a conscious decision to spend whatever I could afford to make this first year without him easier and more comfortable. I'd always hated the cold, so I considered this purchase money well spent.

I felt like I was doing a good job financially speaking. I'd received the check from Steven's life insurance policy. His sizable 401(k) had been transferred into my name as an inherited account. I then met with our financial advisor, who created an investment plan based on my financial goals, and I finally had a closing date set for the sale of our old apartment the following week.

I was acting responsibly and taking care of business.

Wasn't it time for *me* to have some fun?

I was afraid I might be late, but when I got to the restaurant we had agreed on, Jay hadn't arrived yet.

"Excuse me miss, would you like something to drink?" The waiter stood in front of me, proffering a drink menu.

"I'll have a Corona, please."

As the waiter headed back toward the bar, I saw my date walk in.

My first thought was that everything about Jay was average. Average height, average weight, average hair, average clothes. I could have passed him on the street every day and never noticed him.

"I hope you weren't waiting long," he said apologetically.

"No, I just got here," I said, faking a smile.

I hated when people were late. Before Steven died, I might have said something sarcastic like, "No problem, I have all day to sit here drinking by myself," but then I thought that if Steven were alive, I wouldn't have been on this date. Suddenly I felt defeated, and so unsure of myself.

We exchanged a few pleasantries about the weather and then moved on to the get-to-know-you questions.

"What kind of work do you do, Jay?"

I wasn't that into him, but if I was going to throw myself into the dating pool I had to start somewhere.

"I'm an educator at a museum."

I mentally gave him points for working in the arts before I resumed our Q and A. "Nice. I handle the finances for a small grant-making institute at Columbia University's Graduate School of Journalism. Are you from New York?"

"No, I'm from Tampa, Florida, but I've lived here for ten years. And you?"

"From New York, born and raised. How about your family, do you have any siblings?"

"I have a sister and three brothers. Well, two brothers now, one of them died two years ago. Colon cancer."

That got my attention. I already knew he was fifty-three years old, divorced for four years, with dual custody of his two teenage daughters who were still in high school.

He knew I was recently single and that I had a son, but not that I was a widow. I wondered, since he had mentioned cancer, if now was a good time to tell him. It felt like such a big part of my identity at the time, and I felt uncomfortable keeping it a secret.

"I'm so sorry about your brother. I know how devastating cancer can be . . ." I paused and took a swig of my beer before I continued, "So, um, I am recently single because my husband died from soft tissue sarcoma, a rare form of cancer."

I didn't feel it necessary to tell Jay that he and my husband were the same age.

"Oh! Gosh, I am so sorry," he said. "It really does suck. As a matter of fact, I finished treatment for skin cancer on my back six months ago."

I didn't know what to say, so I said nothing.

He was the first to break the awkward silence. "I am totally fine now. The doctor said they got all of it and chemo killed any lingering cells."

Was he trying to reassure me or himself that he wasn't going to die too?

"Oh, I'm so glad you're okay. What a relief!" I said, flashing him my best smile.

But my smile was completely fake. I wasn't concerned about his future because I knew there was no way I would ever see him again. I absolutely could not dive back into cancer-land, no way, no how. We got through the lunch somehow, but I think we both knew there wasn't a connection. Still, I'd dipped my toe into this new world, and I wasn't going to stop now.

My Bumble profile needed a refresh. I wasn't thrilled with my first set of photos, so I took a bunch of selfies in the apartment and a few across the street in Riverside Park. I still needed a photo of my whole body, and I wished I knew how the timer worked on my Android's camera phone. It was past time for an upgrade, and I wanted an iPhone.

I opened my computer and went to the Apple store website. I could hardly believe a new phone would cost me more than a thousand dollars. Then I reminded myself that if it made my life easier and more comfortable, it was worth it. I bought the newest model they had in stock, along with a phone case, and had it delivered later the same day.

Of all the changes I'd made over the last few months, this one felt like the biggest. Was buying an iPhone an insult to Steven's memory? I felt both excited and sad when I would have preferred to feel neutral. I told myself it was only a phone, but there were so many memories attached to it.

As I looked around the living/dining room, I realized that I had already spent thousands of dollars on new furniture: the overstuffed microfiber couch and matching loveseat, the faux marble coffee table, the white pedestal dining room table surrounded by four blue velvet chairs.

While I was proud of the home I'd created, I knew the only reason I had money and freedom to buy what *I* wanted was because Steven had died. If not for him, I wouldn't have had a pot to piss in. He'd been a saver his whole life and had invested his money wisely.

My brain made a case for causation between Steven's death and my financial independence. I did enjoy not having to worry about money, but of course I wasn't happy he had died. He had only been gone for three months, and I missed him terribly. But did that mean I had to feel guilty that he'd left me with money? Should I feel ashamed that I didn't want to feel so lonely? What I was discovering about widowhood was that it was a constant swirl of emotions. One moment I would feel incredibly lonely, the next grateful for my independence to make decisions on my own.

All I knew for sure was that I longed to feel alive again.

Ping!

It was a notification from Bumble; I had a new match. His name was Joel.

I pulled up his profile to refresh my memory and saw that he was a redheaded cutie. He was also thirty-eight years old. I was fifty-four. For a moment the age difference gave me pause, but then I thought, *Fuck it, I don't have to marry him.*

Again, I had to send the first message. Why was it so hard to decide what to write?

"Hey, what are you up to on this fine Wednesday afternoon?"

Ugh Amy, again?

A few seconds later he sent a voice message. I'd never seen that before. Even though I was alone in my apartment I felt the need for privacy. I put on my noise canceling headphones and pressed play.

"Hi, I'm so glad you matched with me. You look cool. I'm doing well, what's going on with you?"

The headphones made it sound like he was standing right next to me, whispering in my ear. His voice was very deep, and I couldn't help thinking he sounded sexy. A man's voice was always a thing with me. It could be neutral, or high pitched and whiny. I remembered the relief I felt when I heard Steven's even tone for the first time.

Before I could decide how to respond, he sent another voice message: "Hey, we should get together. When are you free?"

I took my phone into the most private place in the apartment, my bathroom. How did this voice message thing work? I tapped the microphone icon and said in my sultriest voice, "My schedule is flexible, what's good for you?"

"Wow! I didn't expect you to sound like that, oh man . . ."

He thought I sounded hot! I couldn't help but feel proud of myself. And he sounded hot too. I knew it was sort of petty to judge a man by how he sounded, but who said I was perfect? What I hadn't realized until that moment was how attracted I could be to a man's deep voice. I made a mental note to screen future matches with voice messages.

My mind was racing, and I still didn't know how to respond. An image of Olivia Newton John at the end of the movie *Grease* popped into my head, "Tell me about it . . . stud."

Okay Amy, you can't say that.

"I wasn't expecting your voice to be so deep. I guess we all have our secrets. There are other things about me that are not in my profile either."

This was the most carefree and sexy I had felt in years.

"Oh really? Now I am intrigued," he said mischievously. "I would love to know some of your secrets."

His voice made me feel a desire I hadn't felt in so long, but suddenly I lacked the imagination to tell him anything other than the truth. Yet I didn't want to say that my life had imploded, that everything about my past was gone.

There was no way he could have understood that I used to be somebody's everything, and now I was nobody's anything. I wanted to tell him I was a blank slate, that I could be anyone he wanted me to be, but I couldn't find the words.

I blurted out, "My husband died three months ago. He lived with incurable cancer for three years. I feel like I've been alone for a long time." I hit send.

Nothing.

One.

Two.

Three . . .

He sent another voice message.

"Look, I'm sorry. That's terrible, but it's just a little too heavy for me. This isn't going to work out."

As I stared at my phone, the chat disappeared, and a pop-up message confirmed he had unmatched. I was hurt, but also angry at myself for revealing too much too soon. Maybe it was time to try another dating app. I took a deep breath and walked slowly down the hall and back into the living room.

CHAPTER FIVE

STEVEN'S stepmother was hosting Thanksgiving that year; she alternated with his brother, who had flown in from Seattle with his family. At the last minute I decided not to go even though her apartment was just across town. I couldn't be there without Steven. I had been doing well since Halloween, but I realized I didn't have the capacity to carry the extra emotional weight of another big holiday.

Henry would survive Thanksgiving at home with me. It had never been a big deal in my house growing up. My stepfather was a psychoanalyst who saw patients until 10 p.m. on Thanksgiving. My mother hated turkey, so we celebrated the holiday with Cornish game hens at 11 p.m. and slept until noon the next day.

I wanted to watch the Macy's Thanksgiving Day Parade on TV like I had when I was a kid, but Henry wanted to watch YouTube videos. I kept the parade on in the background while I set up a profile on Tinder.

A coworker I knew had met her husband on the app so I figured it couldn't be all bad. I paid for a month of the premium membership so I could see who liked me, but I was not overwhelmed with my choices until I saw a familiar face . . . Joel.

I took a screenshot and sent it to Lisa with a text, "Look who liked me on Tinder, that guy Joel who blew me off when I told him I was a widow. I'm really tempted to match with him so I could tell him off."

Lisa replied, "You should, what an asshole."

Nah, I shouldn't . . . but what if I did?

It dawned on me that I had already faced my worst fear; my husband died, and I was still here.

I pressed the heart, and I matched with Joel for a second time.

I realized that one of the benefits of living through your worst nightmare was that everything else felt inconsequential and unimportant.

I was disappointed when I realized Tinder didn't have voice messaging.

Amy: I'm surprised you would want to match with me again.

Joel: Oh, hey. Did we match before? Bumble?

Seriously? He didn't remember me?

Amy: I'm the widow you didn't want to have sex with.

I hit send, but was blocked by a pop-up from the Tinder bot: *Hey, slow down! Do you really think your match is ready to hear that?*

I paused for just a second before I pressed send again. This time my message was delivered. I assumed that sex had been the original plan, before I'd told Joel that I was a widow.

Poor baby, I thought sarcastically, *my baggage is too heavy for you to carry—asshole.*

I assumed he would just unmatch again, but he didn't.

Joel: Oh. Sorry about that. I was going through a few things. Do you want to text?

Before I typed a response he sent me his cell number. His area code was within New York City, so he was probably legit. Still, I ran the number through a verification website for confirmation.

Once I had his last name, I typed it into the search field on Facebook. All profile pictures were public, so even if his account was private there might be at least one photo to compare to his Tinder pics. Lucky for me, his account was public and there were plenty of photos to confirm his identity. Satisfied, I texted him, "Hey, it's Amy."

For a moment I wondered if I'd invaded Joel's privacy by investigating his digital footprint, but I quickly reframed my queries as standard recon before I handed over my phone number to a stranger I met on the Internet.

When I ran my own number a week earlier, I was relieved to see it was still listed under Steven's name and connected to our old address. I kept my last name when we got married, so there was nothing linking it back to me.

Joel and I sent a lot of voice messages to each other. I was the one who'd brought sex into the conversation, so I wasn't surprised when it continued in that direction.

Joel: "Do you want to see the uncropped version?"

In one of his profile photos Joel was wearing a Stay Puft Marshmallow Man costume from the movie *Ghostbusters*. It was cut off at the waist, but now he offered a view below the belt.

"Yes please," I said in my most sultry voice.

No one had ever sent me a dick pic before, so I wasn't sure why so many women hated them. I guess it depended on who sent it, and in what context. I guess I would be shocked or scared if it was sent unsolicited by a stranger who intended to shame or frighten me. Otherwise, I didn't see the problem.

This technology didn't exist in 2007 when Steven and I met on J-Date.com. I don't think texting naughty photos was a thing then. Even if guys were doing it, Steven was not. He was quite shy and hadn't lost his virginity until his late twenties. He still carried an image of himself as a nerdy high school student who didn't understand why he couldn't get his shit together and hand in his homework.

I was more experienced sexually, but I liked Steven's innocence. He didn't sexualize me the way other men did, which I appreciated. Before Steven got sick, we had a good sex life. Still, there were times when I wish he had been able to see me as both a person with thoughts and feelings *and* as a sexual being. But I was grateful to have the former, so I didn't push the latter. In addition, being a mom and working full-time left little mental energy for sexual fantasies, so our sex life was never anything out of the ordinary. I also believed we had a long future together and that maybe one day we'd have more time and energy to explore those aspects of our relationship. Now that I knew that life could be ripped away unexpectedly, I was open to exploring and discovering the parts of myself that made me feel more alive, especially sexual pleasure.

I clicked on the picture Joel sent. He wasn't wearing boxers under the flimsy white onesie costume, and his giant boner was pitching a tent over his crotch. I assumed he hadn't left the house looking like that, but I thought he looked adorable.

I couldn't stop staring at the photo and was surprised by the thoughts running through my head. And looking at him now, I didn't care that he was sixteen years younger than me; we were both adults.

At fifty-four years old, I was more self-conscious about my body. I had neglected myself for so long, I wasn't even sure what it looked like anymore. I walked down the long hallway to my bathroom where a full-length mirror doubled as the door to a giant medicine cabinet built into one of the walls.

I stared at my reflection: fitted black jeans and a body-hugging long-sleeved T-shirt. The bathroom's two frosted windows were not insulated so it was colder there than in the rest of the apartment.

Braless, my erect nipples were clearly visible under the stretched light gray material. I snapped a headless selfie of my chest and sent it to Joel. *That'll work,* I said to myself. I had never done anything remotely like this before, and I wondered if I would regret it later. At that moment, though, it felt not only normal, but like the most exciting thing in the world I could do.

I'd had no choice about Steven's cancer diagnosis and his death. I had stayed with him through all of it, doing my best despite my fear and pain, but now, all of a sudden, I did have choices. I could choose how I moved forward.

I wanted to feel free to indulge in what brought me pleasure; hadn't I earned that? To sit still and carry on like I was the same person was not possible. Maybe I was expected to be my normal old self, but she was gone.

No one understood that a part of me had died too, and that the part that was still here didn't give a fuck about being polite. How did people just keep going on with their lives when my husband had been ripped out of mine?

I realized now that anticipatory grief had been my constant companion for three years. The anxiety before each CT scan and the fear of what his death would look like were such heavy burdens. As it all unfolded, I hadn't really noticed exactly how heavy these burdens were, but now that the worst had happened, I felt a sense of relief in having survived. Then I felt so guilty for associating any sense of relief with Steven's death. There was a duality in grief I hadn't expected, and I often felt two or more competing emotions at the same time.

Part of me also felt invincible, not because I believed that nothing bad would ever happen again, as if I'd reached my quota of shitty outcomes and was now exempt from further tragedy, but for the exact opposite reason; I had a deep knowing in my bones that when horrible things did happen, I would survive. My armor had been forged in unspeakable pain.

As time marched forward, I felt a desire to strip it off, piece by piece.

CHAPTER SIX

I WENT BACK to work at the beginning of December when my short-term disability ended, but my department in the Columbia Journalism School still operated 100 percent remotely. Students and faculty had been prioritized back on campus, while administrators were considered "nonessential" workers.

Before Steven died, I had loved my job. I handled budgets and finance for a small institute that made grants to journalists using innovative technology to tell headline-making news stories. I felt gratified to work closely with grantees to help them reach their reporting goals, and I was also grateful my job provided such good health insurance, especially since Steven was diagnosed with terminal cancer one month after I started.

I had been extremely productive while working remotely during the first eighteen months of the pandemic, but that was when Steven was alive. The last few months before he died, we spent our days together at the dining room table. He always had a book in his hand while I tapped the keys on my laptop, and having work to focus on distracted me from the imminent loss that loomed over both of us in those quiet days. Now, I could not concentrate on my job, and I was alone in the apartment all day.

More and more of my time was spent chatting and sexting with Joel. Sexting was an easy way to keep him engaged when

I felt incapable of conversation. Sex was the only way I would allow myself to be truly vulnerable, and his earlier rejection of "widowed Amy" had taught me not to talk about death, loneliness, or my longing to feel connected to another human being.

It had been a long time, at least three years, since I'd felt at all connected to my body and sexuality. Communicating with Joel made me feel like I was coming back to life, reminding me of the carefree, flirty fun I discovered in college.

What would my younger self have done with a smartphone? Better they hadn't existed—I had been in a sorority, and we did our fair share of partying. Still, I was surprised to discover that even though I may not have been nineteen years old anymore, I was still a woman who wanted to be desired and admired.

I had been an art history major and was used to seeing paintings and statues of classical nudes. I never thought they were dirty or subversive. As things unfolded with Joel, I realized that I wanted to see myself that way, too, as a work of art. I wanted Joel to see me that way.

I went into my bedroom, took my shirt off, and laid down on my bed. I held up my phone and snapped a photo of my chest. It was okay, but I wanted artistry. Light, shadow, body position, and contours would work together to create something more than just a picture of breasts.

When I played around with a couple of pillows I realized if I put one or two under the small of my back, I achieved a nice arch. This time the photos looked much better. My arched back lifted my breasts and flattened my stomach.

I wanted to capture my whole body, so I stripped completely naked and lay down on the bed with my head hanging halfway off one side and two pillows under my glutes. I held up the phone and extended my arm far enough so that everything from my smile to my thighs fit in the frame.

These were nice, but I knew I could do better. I put my free hand between my legs, as if cupping my vagina, while altering my position slightly as I continued to take photos. I was happy with most of them, but one was especially well framed. When I texted it to Joel, he loved it just as much as I did.

Steven and I would never have done anything like this, and not just because he was shy. We were all about having a baby after we got married in 2008, and when it didn't happen naturally, fertility specialists advised us to move straight to ART (assisted reproductive technology). We skipped the fun way of trying to make a baby, and it took five rounds of IVF over three years before we had Henry.

By then so much of my identity was tied to being Steven's wife and Henry's mother. Steven was my stability and my security. Deep down, I had believed that if I advocated hard enough for his treatment that he wouldn't die. In my mind, his death made me a failure in addition to being a widow, and I felt untethered without him.

When I wasn't advocating for Steven, I was trying to get Henry back into school full-time. At the tail end of the pandemic, I'd met with public school officials to lobby for children with autism classifications to be prioritized for full-time, in-person instruction. My request was denied, so I hired a special education lawyer and sued the Department of Education for tuition reimbursement at a special needs private school which offered 100 percent in-person instruction. I won my case because by law, every child has the right to a free and appropriate public education.

While I was ecstatic for Henry, I wished I'd had a better outcome for my husband. I knew deep down that I hadn't failed Steven, I wasn't even a doctor. But again, the duality of feelings threatened to overwhelm me. I was proud of my role in getting Henry what he needed, and in the process standing up for others in need of support, but I also felt ashamed of failing to keep my husband alive, the most important task I'd ever put on myself.

Steven had inherited neurofibromatosis, a neurological disorder that caused fatty tumors (almost always benign) to grow on peripheral nerves, from his father. In 2001, six years before we met, a tumor formed in his intestine, which caused him some pain. He didn't see a doctor until he'd almost bled out internally and was hospitalized for three weeks.

When he was first diagnosed with cancer, my fear of losing him exploded in anger. It never occurred to me until after he died that his ADHD may have caused him to hyperfocus on his work while ignoring his body. By the time I saw the tumor on his inner thigh, it was the size of an avocado.

Steven was so stressed out by his new job. His boss was such a dick and verbally abusive. I knew it made him feel like he couldn't do anything right. No matter how many hours he put in, he couldn't keep up with that asshole's deadlines. By the time he went to bed, well past midnight, I would already be asleep.

He'd gotten into the habit of tucking me in and then going back out into the living room to finish his work. With all we had going on with his work and our family there was never much time to see each other naked, let alone think about sex. One night he lifted a side of his boxer shorts to scratch his leg and that's when I saw the tumor. I was so shocked I began yelling at him, screaming, "What the fuck is that?! Have you seen a doctor? What's going on?!"

He looked at me like a scolded child. Did I remind him of his mother? I'd never thought that before, but now I felt a flash of shame and remorse for acting like she had when he was a kid. She'd been a high school teacher back in the 1970s and 1980s, when standards and ambition were prioritized over compassion and awareness of neurodiversity and different learning styles. She thought he was just disorganized and lazy, which seems like a horrible thing to think now, but Steven never blamed her.

He said people didn't know about ADHD back then and couldn't understand how he could be so smart yet do so poorly in school. Still, he'd internalized so many of her criticisms, so many bad feelings, and it had always pained me that he didn't know how wonderful he was. I always tried to tell him, to make him feel like the amazing man he grew up to become. But in that instant, looking at the grotesque protrusion on his thigh, I was horrified. I just flipped out. Fear and anger took over my body and I completely lost it.

I ordered him to see my doctor the following day. He did, and then everything unraveled so fast. An ultrasound led to an MRI which led to a full-body CT scan.

I knew that cancer was suspected, but I also thought the doctors would just cut out the lump and he'd be fine. I was so fucking ignorant. At first, part of me *wanted* it to be cancer so he'd be scared into finally taking care of himself.

But the full-body CT showed ten tumors in one of his lungs and twelve in the other.

How could I have been so stupid? The shame was almost unbearable.

When we got home, I began crying, and I yelled at him.

"We had everything! Now we have nothing!"

He promised he would never ignore medical symptoms again, because Henry and I needed him. I felt betrayed, though; he'd broken his word. I was so focused on what I was losing that I shut him out from the moment of his prognosis. All I could think was, *How could he do this to me? To us?*

CHAPTER SEVEN

THE JOURNALISM School always closed the week between Christmas and New Year's Day, and I was looking forward to the break. I was having trouble concentrating, but there was a real lack of interest in my work too. I needed something to elevate my mood.

"I think I'm going to order a tree. What do you think?" I half yelled over to Henry from the dining area, "I found a great spot for it over here. What do you think? Henry?"

I knew he was parked in his spot on the big couch, probably watching YouTube, but he wasn't in my line of sight. I got up and peeked around the corner to see he was wearing his headphones and hadn't heard anything I said. Oh well, that was okay. I knew he would appreciate a tree—and I knew I wanted one.

This would be the first time I bought my own tree, and I was excited. Growing up we always had a Christmas tree because my mother loved them. As a Jewish girl growing up in Chicago, she wasn't allowed to have one, so when she moved to New York in her twenties it became her new tradition. She kept it going almost every year until she died in December 2018.

We had started spending Christmas with my brother and his family when they moved to a house in the suburbs just before Henry was born. His wife was Christian, and she and her mother went all out with mountains of great food, decorations, and presents. This year would be different, and not only because it was our first without Steven. My brother and his wife had split during the pandemic, and he had moved into an apartment nearby. My allegiance had always been with my brother, but I was heartbroken by their breakup. It felt like I had lost another part of my family.

He and my sister-in-law, as I will always think of her, were still on good terms and wanted to spend one last holiday in the house together with their kids. My niece was already in college and my nephew was graduating from high school in June, so they were putting the house on the market in the spring. I should have been relieved that things would be as normal as possible for Henry, but all I felt was the loss of another part of my family.

"Henry!" I yelled to get his attention.

"What?" He didn't look up from his screen.

"What do you think about getting our own Christmas tree this year?"

"I don't know," he said distractedly.

He acted like he didn't care, but I wanted to make it festive in the apartment. I planned to order a bunch of small indoor lights from Amazon to string around the living room, but that was all the decorating I could handle. I got my laptop from the kitchen island and Googled "Decorated Christmas trees," then found a nearby plant store that could deliver one tomorrow while Henry was in school.

A few days before Christmas my brother called to tell me he and my niece had tested positive for Covid, so the last Christmas at their house was canceled. Instead of being disappointed, I felt relieved. I was happy to skip another family tradition where Steven would be absent. Perhaps that's what had fueled my desire to get a tree for the first time. On some level I must have known after missing Thanksgiving with Steven's family that I wouldn't want to be with any family on a major holiday.

By 8 a.m. on Christmas morning, Henry had already opened all his gifts. I was off from work, and he was off from school until after New Year's Day. I was glad I had the foresight to sign him up for coding camp in the neighborhood for a few days. I'd planned an afternoon rendezvous with Joel later in the week, so I'd need him out of the apartment. I decided to text Lisa to wish her a good day.

Amy: Merry Christmas! Guess who I have a date with next week?

Lisa: Merry Christmas! Joel? Where?

Amy: Yes, we're meeting at my apartment ;)

Lisa: Text me after and tell me everything!

She really was a good friend, and I appreciated her excitement. When we were younger, before we both got married, we always shared updates about our love lives. I loved that it was easy to reconnect on this level so many years later.

When my brother called later in the afternoon, I had a feeling it was bad news about our father, who had been sick. For the last fifteen years, my eighty-six-year-old father had said he wasn't afraid to die because he'd had a good life, but even though I knew he was ill now I also knew I was unable to watch another person I loved take their last breath. My brother was spending time with him instead, although since he'd gotten sick with Covid he hadn't been able to visit. Both of us planned to check in with him later in the day.

I had a bad premonition, but I answered the phone cheerfully anyway.

"Hey, happy holidays."

"Dad died earlier this morning, I'm sorry. I wish I could have been there . . ." his voice trailed off.

"All we need is you being ground zero for a Covid outbreak in an assisted living facility," I said jokingly.

This is the type of relationship I've always had with my brother. We were pragmatic, blunt, and said things other people would scoff at. But we got each other.

"He fucking had to die on Christmas," I continued.

"Yeah, I know," my brother chuckled, "I was thinking the same thing."

We agreed that he would call the funeral home and arrange to have our father cremated. I still had our mother's ashes in a box in my closet, so I told him he got our dad. Eventually I would have Steven's ashes too, once the medical school was done with their studies, although I didn't feel they would provide much comfort. It was also too macabre to imagine living with more dead people I loved than those still alive.

I wanted to rest a bit over the holidays, but with so much responsibility on my shoulders, it was impossible. Since I'd dipped my toe into the dating pool, I'd been thinking that maybe I should create another persona with her own secret life, one that nobody could take away from me. More than ever, I felt the need to be physical with a man, and I was glad Joel would be coming over in a couple of days. I didn't want to think about death anymore. I just wanted someone to bang some life back into me. Was that asking too much?

We got through a nice Christmas dinner of breaded chicken cutlets (one of the few things I cooked), and I checked one more holiday without Steven off my list. Now I could turn all my attention back to myself and my "date" with Joel.

The morning of my rendezvous with Joel was cold and raw. My hands and cheeks were pink from the icy wind, even though I didn't go out for long. I dropped Henry off at coding camp and had six full hours to myself, including an hour and a half to get ready before Joel came by.

I walked down the long hallway to my bathroom and stripped naked, leaning into the rain shower to test the water temperature. I hadn't readied my body for a new man in over fifteen years. Pulling the skin folds between my legs taut, I shaved the area clean and smooth. Next, I lathered my legs from ankle to thigh. First one, then the other, I pulled the razor up in long strokes until each was bare of soap and stubble.

I shaved the hair from each armpit and moved on to exfoliating with a coarse loofah. I began at my toes and worked my way up, scrubbing in clockwise circles past my thighs, butt, back, and breasts. My final step was a full body brown sugar scrub infused with coconut oil that kept my skin soft and hydrated.

The steam from the hot water billowed over the shower's glass door, fogging up the full-length mirror. I rinsed the oily crystals from my body and turned off the water. Pulling my long cotton robe to me, I wrapped it around my body, cinching it tightly at the waist against the chill coming in through the frosted windows.

I walked back into the warmth of my bedroom and turned on the light inside my walk-in closet. It was mostly empty. I'd shed a lot of my clothes and shoes during the pandemic. I was barely going outside, and my twice-a-day Zoom staff meetings meant I could wear anything, or nothing, from the waist down.

There was only one outfit hanging from the longest garment bar, a sexy maid's costume with a headband covered in frilly white lace. I had not bought it at Joel's request, although I hoped it would be a pleasant surprise. I pulled it off the hanger and was struck again by the quality of something I'd bought so cheaply from Amazon two days earlier. I had decided that it would feel easier to pretend I was someone else rather than try to forget that my husband had recently died. I wanted to keep my social life separate from my reality as a widowed mother.

I had never owned anything like that maid's costume before, and I loved it.

CHAPTER EIGHT

IN RETROSPECT, that maid's costume was quite chaste compared to later purchases I'd make, especially because this time I paired it with black kitten heels, the only "dressy" shoes I owned at the time.

The knee-length black jumper was cut under the bodice to reveal the thin white cotton material of the cropped top. Elasticized around the top and bottom, I wore it scrunched up and under my breasts and off the shoulders like an Oktoberfest beer wench. A frilly white apron tied securely at the waist completed the ensemble.

It was an impulse purchase borne out of my dawning understanding of what might turn Joel on. In a world gone a thousand shades of gray, I was grateful for the absoluteness of opposites: black and white, soft and hard, dominant and submissive. I knew my role, and I was ready to play.

Joel and I had been talking and sexting for a couple of weeks and a sense of familiarity had grown between us. Our conversations were often, but not always, explicit. When Joel asked me if he should bring anything for our "date," I sent him a photo of all the snacks in the pantry.

Joel: I was talking about sex toys, but I'm gonna have some of those Welch's Fruit Snacks. I eat them in order, from the worst flavors to the best.

Amy: So do I! I separate them by color and eat the yellow first, then orange, purple, and red last. I think it's cherry.

Joel: Nope, purple is the worst, then yellow, orange, and red. And yeah, it's cherry.

Joel sure knew his Fruit Snacks. I bought them for Henry's lunch; they were the only type of "fruit" he would eat.

Amy: I guess we have to agree to disagree.

Joel: Yeah, but do you want me to bring any sex toys?

Amy: Surprise me. It's my year of living dangerously.

I doubted Joel would catch the reference to the 1982 film starring Mel Gibson and Linda Hunt, about a love affair set in Indonesia during the overthrow of Sukarno. It came out a year before he was born.

Now I looked at the woman in the mirror. "Are you really ready to play?" I asked her.

It would be hard to take her seriously wearing that costume.

"You don't even *have* any sex toys," I said, disappointed.

I wondered what Joel would bring. At least I'd bought lubricant when I ordered the costume.

It had been a long time since I had been intimate with anyone, including Steven. We'd been going through a rough patch even before he was diagnosed with cancer. Once he started chemo, neither one of us really wanted to have sex. We did it maybe twice during his three years of treatment. Possibly three times, but I wasn't keeping track.

Did Steven and I ever have a great sex life? Not really, but great sex was lower on my list of priorities as a forty-year-old woman who wanted some stability and security in her life. I'd had my fair share of great sex. What I hadn't had was commitment.

Ours certainly wasn't a platonic relationship, especially before Henry was born. I bought a vibrator called "The Sure Thing" that I saw on an episode of Oprah about female sexuality and orgasms. It lived up to its name, but we tossed it a year later when the charger mysteriously disappeared, and I never replaced it. We hadn't been using it much anyway. The combination of parenting and work led to the same exhaustion that impacts most couples at some point.

I hadn't thought much about sex once Steven was sick, but now it occupied a lot of my mental space. I was ready for Joel, but there was still half an hour to kill before he would arrive. I walked back down the long hallway, past the enormous kitchen island, and opened the pantry. I took out the large box filled with forty small packets of Welch's Fruit Snacks and poured them into one of Steven's old serving bowls.

At least we would have something to talk about—and we wouldn't go hungry, I thought.

After plugging in the Christmas tree and the string of fairy lights draped around the living room, I turned off the bright overheads to create a cozy atmosphere. I turned slowly, taking an inventory of all the places we could do it: the big couch, the little couch, the coffee table, the shag rug, the kitchen island . . . I supposed at some point we would make it to my room.

The truth was, I had no idea how these next few hours would play out. It's not that we never talked about sex, because we did. Joel suggested I craft a few paragraphs describing exactly what I wanted him to do to me, but I didn't want to.

I was exhausted—all the time. I had to be in control of everything in my life now; all of life's daily admin and taking care of Henry fell solely on my shoulders. I felt like I was being crushed under the weight of it. Was it too much to ask for him to write a few paragraphs?

Apparently, it was.

Joel: If I'm in control, then I'm not going to tell you what I'm going to do ahead of time. You'll have to trust me and have a safe word.

I thought he was probably just being lazy, but I still didn't have it in me to write out instructions for him.

Amy: Do you have a safe word?

I couldn't imagine a scenario where he would need to use one.

Joel: Banana. I like to keep it playful.

Amy: Okay, then my safe word is cherry.

I was both scared and excited at the thought of giving up complete control in the way he was suggesting, something I'd never done before. I didn't think Joel would seriously injure me, but if he slapped me around just a little, maybe I deserved it. If I had been a better spouse, I would have noticed Steven's tumor sooner and he might still be alive.

I also liked having secrets. They made me feel badass and slightly reckless. No one from my old life as Steven's wife would suspect me of having a safe word. They probably didn't even know what that meant. I could be whoever I wanted in this costume, in this apartment that I paid for on my own. I made the rules here.

My knowledge of BDSM was limited, but I watched a few YouTube videos by people who "lived the lifestyle."

The Dominant had the illusion of being in control, but they could not do anything without the Submissive's consent. This appealed to me because I could get out of my head; I wouldn't have to think about anything. I could just submit and let things unfold— safely.

Of course, this arrangement was usually worked out ahead of time; I supposed that's why I had a safe word. I normally had a high tolerance for pain, so I hoped I wouldn't need to use mine. There was also that majorly fucked-up part of me that believed I let Steven die and should be punished. I did have some vague awareness of this belief at that time, but I didn't want to question it then. I just wanted to experience a life that was my own, a life that wasn't so tied to my memories of Steven and who I had been with him. I had no choice but to create a new me, a woman who could navigate the world without being in excruciating pain.

When he rang the buzzer, I took one last look at myself in the mirror before opening the thick metal door into a tiny vestibule the size of a small windowless closet. Two doors there led either to the basement (used as storage) or the short hallway leading to the main entrance of the building.

I buzzed him in, listening for the double slam of the two sets of front doors. Four sets of doors protected me from the chaos of the world outside, but in that moment, I threw them all open and welcomed the insanity inside. I didn't feel nervous, though, or unsafe—I felt strangely exhilarated. Strangely alive.

Joel smiled, his eyes mischievous as he scanned my body from head to toe.

"I like the costume," he said as I stepped aside to let him in.

I was relieved to see he looked just like his profile pictures. He was a little taller than Steven, and bulkier. I took his coat and noticed his wide shoulders and a tight butt beneath his jeans. What a hottie.

He was wearing a loose-fitting sweatshirt, so I could only imagine what was underneath: hard arm, chest, and thigh muscles and washboard abs? His red facial hair matched the short, cropped hair on his head so I assumed he would be a real redhead below the waist too.

Damn, he looked young. I couldn't tell if he really did have a baby face or if I was just hyperaware of our sixteen-year age difference. His nose was long and straight, and I imagined his ancestors were Dukes or Earls. He had a high forehead, but without a hint of a receding hairline. His lips were full and pink, without a trace of femininity. What would he do to me if I bit the lower one? It wasn't easy for me to hold back, but I knew enough about the game we were playing to understand that he had to be the one to take the lead.

I offered him a seat on the small couch while I sat on top of the coffee table opposite him. I looked down and noticed a medium-sized duffle bag at his feet. I wondered what he had in there. I felt a shiver of anticipation just thinking about it.

CHAPTER NINE

OUR CONVERSATION came easily, and we both talked openly about our families. I thought our time together would play out like a video from Porn Hub, where I would open the door in my maid's costume, we'd have some meaningless dialogue, and then get naked. Instead, we had a deep conversation about grief.

In the four months that I had been a widow, I'd noticed that people suddenly felt comfortable confiding in me. I often felt grateful that they trusted me with their painful stories, even though they usually started with a qualifier, "This is nowhere near the level of grief that you've experienced. I'm not even comparing, but this is what happened to me."

It's human nature to compare, contrast, and rank everything, including our life experiences. It helps us know our place in the world and creates a sense of order to the randomness of life. My husband's death had a minimizing effect on other people's losses, which I thought made it easier for people to share with me. Generally, I appreciated when people shared—it made me feel less alone.

I would never tell Joel, but my first thought was that the story he shared about his own grief sounded worse than what I had been through. Then I felt guilty because Steven had died, and wasn't that always the bigger tragedy? Maybe I was trying to minimize my loss too? It never occurred to me that Joel would have a rough backstory, because to me he was just a hot guy with a sexy voice.

In this case, I wished he hadn't confided in me. I didn't want to feel emotionally close to him because I knew that our relationship was just supposed to be about sex. I felt so lost and lonely that I knew it would be easy to "catch feelings" for him. My head was looking for a physical connection, but my heart had been broken open and was looking for love.

I caught a glimpse of the microwave clock and saw that it was already past noon. I didn't think we could just have anonymous sex now that I knew so much about him. I also knew that if I wanted to get laid, we had better get started now.

"All that responsibility shouldn't have fallen solely on your shoulders," I said, thinking about how awful it must have been for him growing up with an alcoholic parent.

"Hey, it's okay, I'm good with it," he answered unconvincingly.

"Well, I think you've played the hero, and heroes deserve to be rewarded," I said as I stood up in front of him.

I felt masterful, like a sixteenth-century Venetian courtesan.

He sat up on the front edge of the couch and I pushed him back into the deep pile of blue pillows. He looked up at me, at first surprised, but then the corners of his mouth turned up into that mischievous grin from his photos. He put his hands on my waist as I braced my right and then my left knee on either side of his legs, straddling him.

He pulled me into a slow, sensuous kiss, and I remembered that I was supposed to let him take the lead. I was dressed as a maid after all. Reaching for his belt buckle, I asked, "May I help you undress?" He nodded, reclining even deeper into the couch cushions. I worked quickly and efficiently, unbuckling his belt and then unbuttoning his jeans. He used his legs to raise his ass off the couch so I could pull his pants down.

The feel of his erection straining between my legs pushed all other thoughts away. I smelled the lingering sweetness of fruit snacks on his warm breath and felt his strong hands on my waist. I was fully present, living in the moment for the first time in months, maybe even years. There was no past to long for, no lost future to mourn, just what was happening between us right at that moment.

Still kissing, Joel pivoted us over the couch, lowering me down onto my back. Up on his knees, arms braced on either side of me, he leaned in to kiss my lips, my cheek, my neck. The elastic in the collar of my white cropped top made it easy for him to slip it off my shoulder and down, until my right breast was exposed.

I closed my eyes as he took my nipple in his mouth, alternating between sucking and gently nibbling. He was teasing me, his movements slow and deliberate, and I knew he wanted me to ask, or maybe beg, for more. I felt confident in my body and my ability to please, so I did.

"Please baby, I need to feel you in me."

He stopped and my eyelids blinked open. As I looked up, he stood, extending his right hand down to me. I grabbed it like a lifeline as he pulled me to my feet. Reaching past me with his free hand, he picked up the duffle bag (I had forgotten about it, but now I was curious) and I led him down the long hallway to my bedroom. I knew my behavior was risky, but I trusted my instincts that he wasn't a dangerous man.

He stopped me at the threshold, swung the duffle bag over his left shoulder, and pulled me to his right side. In one swift movement he lifted me off my feet and carried me like a baby over to the bed. I was a little afraid he was going to throw me onto it, so I was relieved when he put me down gently.

I wasn't sure what to do so I watched as he finished undressing himself. Once naked, I could see that he was indeed a redhead below the waist. He caught me staring and laughed. "I guess it's been a while since you've seen one of these," he said, grabbing his erection in one hand. I felt a little embarrassed because it was true, but I didn't look away.

He bent over, unzipped the duffle bag, and pulled out the largest vibrator I'd ever seen. I assumed it was a vibrator, although it looked like it could knead a knot out of my back.

"Is there an outlet behind the bed?" he asked.

I was wondering why he didn't charge it before he came over, but then I saw it was meant to be plugged in. I stood up on my bed and looked behind my tall headboard. I knew there must be an outlet close by because a TV was meant to be hung on this wall.

"Yes, it's here. I'll plug it in," I said, reaching out my hand. As he placed it in my outstretched palm, I realized it wasn't as heavy as I imagined. *Probably because it doesn't require batteries,* I thought. Once I had plugged it in, I turned to hand it back to him, but he was putting on a condom. I was glad that he brought his own. While I had made sure to stock up on my favorite lube, I hadn't bought any protection. Being post-menopausal I didn't have to worry about pregnancy, and I assumed Joel had a preferred style and brand for STI prevention. There was at least a dozen different types of Trojans alone, and I worried he might be offended if I chose incorrectly.

I had heard stories about other widows crying the first time they had sex with a new person after their partner died, but there was no chance of that happening to me. I was both nervous and excited as he took the vibrator out of my hand and asked me to lay on my back. He moved as if to take off my panties, but I wasn't wearing any.

"Where's your lube?" he asked.

"My bedside table," I said, turning my head to look at the clear plastic bottle with a pump dispenser. He reached over me and squirted two pumps of the clear goop into the palm of his right hand, smeared a glob on my bare labia, and turned on the vibrator. It felt good but was a little faster than I was used to. It wasn't unpleasant, but I was beginning to remember that sex wasn't usually that great with someone the first time. Our sexting had been fantasy; we didn't know each other's specific preferences, and he hadn't wanted to discuss it ahead of time anyway.

Before I reached orgasm he stopped and flipped me over onto all fours. *Finally, we're getting to the main event,* I thought. This felt like progress. I could check one more "first time" since Steven died off my list. I was happy about taking another step toward reinventing myself.

I felt him trying to push inside me, but I was too tight and dry. I felt embarrassed, but he just reached over for more lube. "It has been a while for you," he said, "I can tell." He pushed harder and he was inside me. I laughed; I was so relieved that my vagina still worked.

I felt my body relaxing into his slow thrusts when suddenly, he slapped my right ass cheek hard. This had never happened to me before—I had never felt anything like it. I was startled, but the pain felt surprisingly good. I felt it again on the left cheek, but that slap sounded different.

I turned my head to look behind me and I saw that he was holding a black leather flogger. It was about the size of a small tennis racket, something a child might have used when learning how to hit a ball.

Slap! Slap! One ass cheek was getting flogged, the other slapped. It sounded like it would be very painful, but I wasn't experiencing it that way. I couldn't say it was sexually arousing, but the discomfort kept me focused on the present. My thoughts anchored, I was unable to wander into a past I could not change or the ambivalence I felt about the future.

After a few minutes the slaps stopped, and he changed his position, so he thrusted inside me at a downward angle. That's when I began to feel pain, as he was hitting up against my cervix. It was lower since I'd had a baby, but he was also on the larger side of average, although not freakishly so.

"Cherry!" I yelled, and he immediately stopped. I'd tried so hard to just ride it out, but the pain became too intense.

"I'm sorry!" he said as I turned over onto my back.

He looked worried, so I said, "I'm okay, really. That was just a bad angle for me."

"Really?" He looked confused. "I thought that was the angle to hit your G-spot."

"Every woman's body is different," I said casually. I didn't want to make him feel dumb. "I'm fine, really," I assured him again. "Let's finish up."

I motioned for him to come closer, and we began to kiss. I liked the intimacy of the missionary position; I liked seeing his face as he came inside me. I felt happy, almost giddy.

People who knew me as Steven's wife would be shocked if they knew how I spent my afternoon. I didn't even care that I didn't orgasm; I hadn't expected to after so much time spent disconnected from my body and my pleasure.

As he dressed and gathered up his toys, I reflected on the afternoon. Overall, I thought it had gone well. I was still alive, mostly unharmed, and I'd gotten laid.

I didn't know if I was becoming someone new, or if I was reconnecting with long forgotten parts of my core self. One thing I did know was that I wanted to spend another afternoon with Joel.

I was horrified when I saw my ass cheeks later. They were almost completely black and blue, the left side marginally worse than the right. Standing with my ass facing the bathroom mirror, I took a photo over my shoulder and sent it to Joel.

Joel: Oh man! You took a beating! Awesome!

"Awesome? What the fuck is wrong with him?" I said out loud.

It didn't hurt, but it looked awful, not awesome. It never occurred to me that I would be this banged up. I figured I'd have some red marks, a palm print, maybe a welt, but not be covered in deep purple bruises. It made me feel ugly.

It had only been a few days since we'd been together, but it was a whole new year. He'd celebrated New Year's Eve with friends, but I was surprised and hurt that he hadn't even thought to send me a text or voice message wishing me a happy 2022.

This was my first New Year's Eve without Steven, but all I was thinking about was Joel and my own loneliness.

When he left my apartment, I thought for sure we would see each other again. Maybe we would be "friends with benefits." Or did I want something more? The thought of losing this nascent connection with him felt almost unbearable. I wasn't sure I could survive another person leaving me.

I left him a voicemail, "Don't you feel sorry at all?" I tried to keep my voice steady, but it came out whinier than I wanted it to. I pressed send anyway. I worried if I recorded it again it would sound worse.

He replied, "No, and I don't appreciate you trying to make me feel guilty. If you weren't enjoying it, you should have told me to stop sooner."

I replayed the voice message again and heard a hardness in his voice that made me want to cry. I was frustrated and hurt, but what did I expect?

I wanted to tell him I was sorry, and that of course he didn't do anything wrong. I felt panicked, like I was losing access to the only piece of joy I'd had in months. Before I could respond, he sent another voice message:

"I cannot be your everything, you need to have experiences with other guys. I should have stuck with my first instinct. We are not good together; I'm ending this now."

I sat down on the floor in my bathroom and cried long and hard. I thought I'd found someone who would care about me, but now I had no one. I felt the terrible ache of loss in a way I hadn't even experienced when Steven died. I was ashamed that I hurt so deeply, which only added to the pain.

I didn't know it then, but this more immediate loss was the only way I could access my grief about Steven's death. I hadn't really been able to mourn him properly because I had to take care of Henry, managing all his physical and emotional needs along with supporting him through processing his grief. Anything I was feeling was too dangerous to access. But the afternoon with Joel had given me a window into my own emotions, my own needs. My own horrible sense of loss.

Although I'd gotten what I wanted in terms of the sexual connection, my fear of another loss had been dialed up to eleven.

CHAPTER TEN

JOEL'S REJECTION stung, and knowing I wouldn't see him again left me unmotivated to shower or get out of my pajamas for a few days.

Lisa: Just checking in. Feeling any better?

Amy: Meh.

Lisa: Text if you need anything. I'm so sorry Joel turned out to be such a jerk.

Once again, I was grateful for Lisa's presence in my life. If I didn't have anything else to comfort me or offer me joy right now, at least I had her unwavering support and loyalty.

For once I was glad for early January's frozen temperatures because my full-length puffer hid everything I wore underneath when I walked Henry to and from school. I could no longer pull myself together enough to pack his lunch *and* get dressed in the morning.

I finally opted for a bubble bath in the large soaking tub, and I remembered how easy it had been to take care of my body when I was getting ready to be with Joel. I thought about how motivated I felt to wash my hair when I knew I would be putting on makeup and wearing something that made me feel beautiful.

The maid's costume still hung in my closet. I felt sexy and desirable when I wore it, free from the heaviness of grief and single parenthood. Like any good costume, it transported me out of my life and into a role I could play.

I was tired of being sad, feeling unwanted and discarded. I wondered what other naughty costumes I could buy. I had never owned sexy lingerie before, the kind that served no other purpose than to be sensual. But now it felt as if a miraculous gateway out of grief-ville had opened in my closet, and I was curious and eager to see where it led.

Instead of getting dressed after the bath, I put on the maid's costume and took some selfies of my reflection in the full-length mirror. It was fun to try out different poses and angles. I tried to capture the essence of a naughty maid by grinning while biting down on the nail of my pointer finger. My eyes looked wide and mischievous, as if I had just done something I shouldn't have. It was a great picture.

If a picture is worth a thousand words, I didn't know whether this one told the naughty maid's story, or mine.

The next day I gave Tinder another try, but this time I went into it with an open mind. There must be other types of connections beyond the binary, something in between a long-term heterosexual relationship and a one-night stand. I wasn't necessarily looking for monogamy again, but I hoped there was something that felt a little safer, where I didn't become emotionally invested in another man who would leave me.

I still had my premium membership so I could see who had already liked me, and I noticed Casey, a ballet dancer who was my age. He looked boyish for a guy in his fifties, with a full head of dark, wavy hair. He was wearing a large crystal on a gold chain, which was a little New Agey for my taste. I'd left that behind in the 1990s and I wasn't going back.

Still, I chose to match with him because there was something in his profile I was curious about. Unlike Joel, Casey wanted to talk in real time on a call, so we exchanged numbers. The only other person who shared this preferred mode of communication was my brother. I guessed it was a Gen X thing.

I liked Casey. He was friendly and kind, open and empathetic. If he lived a little closer, we may have become friends, but for now I wanted to ask him about ENM, which was listed on his profile.

I understood the definition of ethical nonmonogamy, but I wanted to ask him how it worked in *real life*. Was it enough that all parties knew about each other, or were there discussions before each sexual experience?

More than anything else, I was drawn to the word ethical. That word hinted at an awareness of other people's feelings. I didn't want to get hurt again, even though the nonmonogamy part was completely foreign to me. We had a phone call about it:

Casey: Amy, there's no "one size fits all" when it comes to relationships. ENM relationships are no different. Each person has to clearly communicate what they want, what they will tolerate, and what is completely off the table.

Amy: What if I felt like I wasn't emotionally available, but I didn't want to go through the winter alone? I'm not looking for a long-term relationship, but I do want monogamy. Is that possible?

Casey: Amy, everything is possible with human relationships. It's just a matter of getting in the right room with like-minded people. Have you been on Feeld?

Amy: Playing the field?

Casey: No, it's a new dating app for people who aren't looking for conventional relationships. It's a little glitchy, but I like it because people are open and honest about what type of connection they're looking for.

Amy: F-I-E-L-D?

Casey: F-E-E-L-D, he corrected me.

Feeld marketed itself as a "dating app for the curious" (translation: kink-friendly), and after what happened with Joel, I thought I qualified. I struggled writing my bio, though, and debated especially hard about whether I should include that I was a widow with a nine-year-old son. Eventually I chose to be brutally honest about everything—except my name.

Cherry*—54, Woman, Straight, Single*

Recently widowed single mom in NYC seeking like-minded, non-partnered man to pair with monogamously for a few weeks or months, to get through the cold winter, early nightfall, and isolation of working remotely at home. I'm emotionally unavailable, but very loyal and trustworthy.

I felt like I had become a pro on Tinder, but I didn't really understand how Feeld worked. There were the regular "likes" and then something called "pings." Was that a super-like? If I had gotten any, I couldn't find them. I became frustrated past the point that the situation merited, so I closed the app and turned off notifications.

I dropped Henry off at school later that morning, but when I got home, I still had a hard time concentrating on work, as usual. It had only been a day since I set up my Feeld profile, but

I was curious to see if I had garnered any interest, so I opened it up. *Whoa!* I had five hundred likes and thirty pings!

The thrill at my popularity dimmed a bit when it became obvious that many of the men had not read my bio. I saw men looking for couples, groups, MMF, MFF, and many other acronyms I didn't understand. I soon realized I needed to keep a tab open for the Urban Dictionary.

I was surprised by how many men in their twenties were interested in me. I couldn't wrap my head around sleeping with someone who was closer to my son's age than mine. I decided that thirty-five was my cut off; even that felt young to me.

I looked at the guys who had pinged me first since I'd figured out that a ping was the equivalent to a super-like. None of them appealed to me until I saw Edward. He looked so much like Joel that at first, I thought it was Joel. They were even the same age, thirty-eight.

No, of course it wasn't really him, I chastised myself. *He didn't want to have anything to do with you, Amy.* I tried not to let any bad feelings I still had about being rejected overtake my curiosity.

I'd never had a type, but suddenly I was really into redheads. Or maybe I was just trying for a better outcome with Joel's lookalike (my therapist would call this a "corrective experience"), but in the end what did it matter? Any man who read my profile would know I wasn't open to an emotional connection.

No one was ever supposed to get hurt in this dating game. In an ideal world, I would have kept my emotions divorced from my sex life, but now I wasn't so sure I had full control over my feelings. It hadn't occurred to me that I would form an attachment to Joel so quickly. It was as if my brain and my body were no longer on speaking terms. My head wanted someone to keep me company, but my heart was screaming, *Please don't leave me!*

I vowed to act more intentionally, no attachments this time around. I hit the like button to match with him and thought, *Okay, Edward, let's see what you're all about.*

I was grateful I didn't have to start the chat first. If he messaged me by tomorrow, I would respond, but if he didn't I would just unmatch. Easy peasy, right?

CHAPTER ELEVEN

WITHIN FIVE minutes of matching with Edward, he sent me a message.

Ed: Hi, it's Ed. How are you, Cherry? Your profile caught my eye because I know what it's like to lose someone you love. It really messed me up, and I just wanted to make sure you were okay.

Amy: Hi Ed, I'm okay. Sorry to hear you lost someone too. It sucks being alone all the time.

Ed: I know. It's been four years for me. In some ways it gets better, but the pain is always there. I can relate to being emotionally unavailable, you aren't alone.

I wanted to believe him that I wasn't alone. We exchanged numbers, and I verified his identity. Ed preferred WhatsApp to texting but liked sending voice messages too. His voice wasn't as deep as Joel's, but it wasn't high pitched or whiny either.

Ed was a travel writer, which I thought sounded cool. He also lived in Brooklyn Heights, which was inconvenient unless he came over to my place. He was cute, smart, had a degree in philosophy, and owned a car.

He said he usually did one or two big trips a year, a month each where he would travel to several countries. While he was a freelancer, he did a lot of work for a well-known magazine, which was sending him to the Nordic countries in the spring.

Ed: I'll be around for the rest of the winter. I may do a little US travel, but that would only be for long weekends here and there. For the most part I'm in town until April.

Amy: Okay, that sounds good. Are you around during the day this week? I can only meet while my son is in school, so usually 9 a.m. to 2:30 p.m.

Ed seemed nice enough, but we agreed to meet at my place in a couple of days for a "vibe check." That seemed to be a normal operating procedure to start a relationship in which sex wasn't considered transactional. If he got here and we didn't have chemistry, we didn't have sex. This felt safe and comfortable to me and alleviated any concerns I had about being pressured to do something I didn't want to do.

So far, I liked Feeld because it attracted men who were clear about what they wanted. I had been clear in my bio about what I was looking for—casual and consistent companionship—and Ed understood that. I told him I wanted someone who would be available for the winter, not just for sex, but to chat with during the day.

What I really wanted was someone to hold me while I cried, but I would never ask for that. I was scared my vulnerability would drive away any potential man who knew this about me, and I didn't want to drive Ed away before we had even met. I also didn't think he would want to be reminded of his early grief, especially since he had admitted that even four years after his loss, he was still emotionally unavailable.

I wanted to keep things fun, so I was excited to look on Amazon for another sexy outfit and some lingerie. They didn't have a huge selection of costumes, but I found a naughty schoolgirl outfit that was available for next-day delivery. It came in a variety of tartan colors, but I went with the classic red uniform: short skirt and halter top with capped sleeves.

There was a better selection in the sexy lingerie department, although some of the pieces were no more than a swatch of lace and some elastic straps. I chose a red teddy, a black lace bodysuit, some black thigh-high stockings, and a five pack of crotchless panties in a variety of colors. None of it was high end stuff, and all together it cost less than one hundred dollars.

My Amazon packages didn't arrive until after 4 p.m. the following day, so I waited until Henry was asleep to try everything on. I brought my bounty into my bathroom since the full-length mirror and the lighting were perfect. When I held up the red teddy there was so little of it that I didn't know how to put it on. I eventually figured it out by looking at the model wearing it on the Amazon listing.

The front consisted of two lace panels connected to an adjustable g-string bottom. It fit well and made me feel sexy and desirable. It also gave me back a little bit of the confidence I lost when Steven died. I hadn't needed to buy all this sexy stuff when he was alive because he made me feel loved and appreciated. We may not have had a red-hot sex life, but I knew he thought I was beautiful. Henry and I were his life, and I never doubted where I belonged.

In some ways it felt like my old life with Steven had ended years ago, but I still remembered his death like it was yesterday—I thought about it almost daily. Still, as I looked in the mirror, I didn't see Amy "the wife." I saw Amy "the widow," and she was a super sexy single woman. I took a bunch of photos of myself in the mirror, some facing front and some from behind.

I was in pretty good shape, but I'd lost muscle tone in the last couple of years and there was some cellulite on my butt and thighs. I was never big into sports or working out, but before the pandemic I walked a lot. Still, although I was home most of the time now, I knew I'd managed to continue looking great.

But I wanted to create pictures that went beyond great, pictures that were beautiful and sensual. There was more to that than just snapping away in the hopes I'd get a good shot. I considered lighting, how to position my body, and my facial expressions as I looked directly into the camera. I wanted to share my photos with someone who would appreciate them as art, but I also wanted to be desired, visible, and seen as a woman.

These photos began to serve as a visual diary for me at a time when I had so much trouble concentrating on reading and writing. They allowed me to express my thoughts and feelings creatively when my words wouldn't form sentences in a journal, something I'd kept on and off since I was a teenager. As time went on, I felt compelled to take these images as documentation of my life, scared my menopause brain fog was incapable of retaining vital information.

It was a little past midnight when I got into bed that night. I was just about to turn off the light when my phone began vibrating. It was Ed video calling on WhatsApp. I debated if I should ignore it because I was makeup free and wearing my glasses, but my curiosity made me answer.

"Hey, I just wanted to say goodnight. I hope it's not too late."

He was sitting up in bed, the covers over his lap like mine were, except he was shirtless.

"No, it's fine," I said tentatively. I wondered why he was calling.

He looked relieved, "Oh good. I'm looking forward to seeing you tomorrow."

"Me too." I didn't know what else to say.

"Okay, good," he paused before continuing, "I wanted to make sure you are still okay with me coming over. I know your loss was recent and I feel a little protective of you."

"I'm good," I said smiling. He seemed genuinely concerned and it felt nice to have him looking out for me. Was this the "boyfriend experience"?

"Great, sweet dreams."

"You too."

The following day I wore the red teddy under my robe when Ed arrived. He looked so much like Joel it was uncanny, but he seemed older, surer of himself. Perhaps grief had aged him, but my background checks verified they were the same chronological age.

This encounter had a totally different vibe from start to finish. His call the night before served as an ice breaker so when I opened my front door, I went straight in for a kiss. After a few seconds he pulled back.

"Let's slow down, we have all morning."

He took my hand, and I led him inside the apartment.

"I'm sorry, I didn't mean to rush you."

I wondered if I had already fucked up, but he said, "No, not at all. We're good. I wasn't sure if I got here too early since you're still in your bathrobe."

I smiled and slowly untied the belt. The robe fell open, and it slid off my shoulders and onto the floor.

We locked eyes for a moment and then he stepped forward to kiss me. It was a slow, tender kiss, very unlike what I experienced with Joel. I led him to my bedroom, and we had sex for a couple of hours. He came prepared with condoms, his preferred size and style, and I decided it didn't make sense for me to stock up on something generic—if a man planned to fuck me, he'd bring the protection of his choice. If he didn't, he was out of luck, and so was I.

This time I got doubly lucky because Ed made sure I orgasmed too, even though the sex was vanilla. After what happened with Joel, I was fine with something more traditional, but I hoped there would be room to spice things up a little in the future. We spent some time chatting in bed afterwards and then it was time for me to pick up Henry. I walked him a block to his car since it was on my way to the school.

"I'll see you soon, babe."

His voice was so sincere; I didn't doubt that I would see him soon.

"Bye babe, see you soon."

When I returned home with Henry, I sent him a quick voice message:

"Thank you for a beautiful morning, Ed."

I felt so happy we connected, but then I didn't hear from him for two days.

My mind went to the worst places. At first, I thought he must be dead, and I felt myself panicking well out of proportion to what was happening in real life. I wasn't in control of my thoughts anymore, and a narrative played in my head that everything was a lie.

Then I began to think he'd been messing with my emotions the whole time. *How fucking dare he!* It wasn't rational, but I was beyond reason. I felt vulnerable and alone, but rage was the only emotion I could process. I left him another voice message:

"Fuck you, motherfucker! Don't you ever fucking come near me or my son again! I will tell your sister what you are up to, you fucking asshole!"

Sometimes too much information is a bad thing, because my verification process always included the names of close family members.

He texted me back immediately:

"Classic trauma response. Read some philosophy and get help."

And then he blocked me.

CHAPTER TWELVE

JANUARY WENT out the same way it came in, frozen solid, but I wasn't bothered by the cold. I wondered whether it was because of my puffer coat, or if I was just developing a thicker skin, both literally and figuratively. I was pleasantly surprised that I'd been able to move on from Ed much faster than from Joel.

Ed's silence had fueled my rage, but once I got his text it drained out of me as quickly as it had burst forth. I was also a little embarrassed at my loss of control and eager to put some distance, and another body, between us.

February was supposed to be the month for love, but it turned to lust when I saw Matt on Feeld. Omg, he was gorgeous, and he liked me! His features were classically handsome, like Brad Pitt's or Tom Cruise's, with a square jaw and straight nose. His slightly wavy light brown hair was cut just above his ears, a little longer in the front. I was relieved he wasn't another redhead.

His face alone would have been enough to grab my attention, but what made him spectacular was his body. In two different photos he was on a beach in just swim trunks. Free of body hair, I could see every cut in his six-pack abs. Swoon!

His bio said he was thirty-seven, so probably he was really in his forties. Either way, I didn't care. I immediately liked him back, so we matched, but then I felt too nervous to start the chat. Within five minutes, though, he sent me a message, "Hey, how are you?"

I typed back the usual, "I'm great, how about you?"

"I'm good. Do you want to text? This app is really glitchy," he typed.

I gave him my number and immediately felt the vibration notifying me I had an iMessage.

Matt was the opposite of Ed, but also different from Joel. He was one 100 percent raunchy sex god; I lost myself over the next three hours chatting and then swapping the most intimate photos of ourselves.

Amy: I'm at the bottom of the bed on all fours and you're fucking me from behind.

Matt: I would love to tease you by rubbing my cock tip on your clit. Do you have full lips?

Amy: Yes, they're plump and juicy.

Matt: I can't wait to rub my shaft between them.

I already had a few photos in my archive from my time with Joel, but there were more I took on the spot. There was something about Matt that unleashed the animal in me. I had no other way to describe it. That day I didn't get any work done, and before I knew it, I had to go pick up Henry from school.

We agreed to reconnect later that night when I suddenly realized I hadn't run a background check on his number. Fuck. I was so engrossed in his body that I'd let it slide. I wasn't overly worried because up to this point everyone had been who they said they were.

I had just enough time to do a reverse phone lookup and . . . it was a Google Voice number. People used them when they wanted to hide their real mobile number.

My mind immediately locked onto a scenario where he tried to extort me for money. I imagined he might try to figure out where I worked then send the photos to my boss. When I played that out in my mind, I was not that upset. My boss might have been shocked, but he wouldn't have fired me.

Still, I felt so vulnerable, because I didn't know what he planned to do with the photos, if anything. I felt paranoid that I had fallen into a trap for reasons I couldn't understand. I began to feel angry and vengeful about something that hadn't even happened yet. I tried to slow down and not panic, but even a few deep breaths failed to calm my fight or flight survival response.

How could I figure out who he really was?

I couldn't let it go, but in hindsight, I should have.

It was still hard for me to manage my emotions, and before I even realized what was happening, I felt rage explode to the surface again, just like it had with Ed.

Fucking Matt, if that's even his real name. How dare he fuck with me!

As I was working through my emotions about all of this, Henry was on the couch in the room with me, so I couldn't lose my cool. I took a few more deep breaths to steady myself. All I could think was that the only reason someone would use a Google Voice number was to hide their identity, and that the only reason they would want to hide their identity was because they wanted to fuck with someone. We would see about that, asshole.

My internal bravado was masking some serious doubts about my ability to figure out who "Matt" really was. He hadn't given me any identifying information, unless I could match his dick pics to a porn site. Haha Amy, you're hilarious. . . .

Then I remembered I'd taken a couple of screenshots of Matt's profile pictures to send to Lisa. Ugh, now I wished I hadn't sent them. Still, they might serve a purpose. It was a long shot, but there was a background-checking website that focused on catfishing. It had a photo lookup option like what Google offers, but for a couple of dollars, it could do an advanced search.

It wasn't NSA-level facial recognition software, but it was worth a try. For a moment I wondered if I was losing my mind. What was I doing? Was I going too far to invade this man's privacy? How did I know he wasn't who he said he was? Was I acting paranoid? My mind raced with questions, but I knew that emotionally, I needed to feel as safe as possible within this dating world.

I hit submit on one of his photos. It took a minute, but then results started to filter in. They were just comps of random shirtless white guys, not exact matches. Same thing with the next photo. Fuck, this was never going to work. I began to wonder if I knew anyone connected with Homeland Security.

I tried for a third time, readying myself for disappointment, but this time the search found an exact match. I could hardly believe what I was seeing on the screen. It was Matt's profile photo, where he was standing in front of a Christmas tree wearing gray dress pants and a crisp white button-down shirt. His clothes were Brooks Brothers or another high-end brand.

There was nothing remarkable or unique about the photo to indicate why the recognition software could distinguish it from other hot guys standing in front of Christmas trees, until I took a closer look. That was when I saw it. This photo had appeared in a magazine article, but it wasn't about him.

It was about his wife.

Turns out Matt was his real name.

The photo had been taken a year ago at their house in a suburb of New York. His wife was a successful jewelry designer; one of her pieces went viral on social media after a celebrity was seen wearing it, which was part of why they had been profiled in the magazine. He was an architect. They had three young children, a daughter and twin boys. I could not help myself and Googled both of them.

There was a lot more information about her, but I did find his very public Facebook page. Why would he have taken that stupid risk? I wondered about his behavior but then realized mine had been perilous too.

I decided it didn't matter why he cheated on his wife; I just knew that given how easy he was to find, he was going to get caught eventually. I thought about him losing it all: his home, his kids, his family, his life as he knew it. I knew what it was like to lose everything. My world had imploded when Steven died. It's true that I didn't have any control over that, and if he lost the things that mattered to him it would have been because of his own bad choices. Still, I didn't wish that on this man.

The anger drained from my body, and all I felt was sadness for those little kids who were going to lose their daddy. I felt like everything was spinning out of control. I'd told Matt that I was a widow, so he knew Henry was growing up without his father. Didn't he understand his kids shouldn't have to go through the same heartache? I wondered if there was anything I could do to stop that from happening.

Later that night, after Henry fell asleep, I texted Matt:

"I know who you are. Stop being an idiot and make your Facebook account private. Right now, any random person can see and comment on your posts. I would *never* do that. You got lucky that I'm a mom first, and my desire to protect your family, especially your innocent kids, is more important than any anger or bad feelings I have toward you. I think my heart is more broken for my son who doesn't get to grow up with a dad. I've already lost everything, but you don't have to."

I never expected to hear from him again. What did it matter anyway? Even if he read my message, it wouldn't change anything. People could not understand what it felt like to lose their person until it happened to them. Until Steven died, I certainly never could have imagined what it felt like to be left alone by the person you loved the most. I felt like an idiot, but at least I was trying to help his children.

It was late, and I was exhausted. Post-adrenaline rush, my eyelids heavy with sleep, I reached to turn off my bedside lamp. That's when I heard my phone vibrate. I had a new iMessage:

"You're right. Thank you. My family is everything to me."

It could have ended there, but somehow it didn't. It was clear to me that I wasn't interested in a future with Matt, even if he had been single. But I also recognized he was dissociating from pain just like I was. An oft said phrase within the grief community is, "Grief is love with no place to go." Assuming that was true, on some level I believed I could circumvent grief by finding a new place for my love to go, which meant a new man to love. I didn't realize it at the time, but in retrospect it's clear that I threw my love at other men hoping it would eventually stick to someone, and I wouldn't have time to mourn my dead husband.

As my relationship with Matt progressed, I realized that being with him felt emotionally safe because he would never be mine to lose. I knew there was no possibility of building a future with him because if he cheated on his wife, of course he would cheat on me too. Better he deceived her while I enjoyed the excitement of our forbidden connection.

As I moved forward with our relationship, I reasoned that I was protecting Matt. If he wasn't cheating with me, he would be doing so with someone else. What if she figured out he was married and told his wife? I convinced myself that my motivation in continuing our relationship was about keeping his family intact, but even if that wasn't entirely true, I decided that the lies he told his spouse were worse than the lies I was using to justify my moral failings.

After all, Matt was the one cheating, not me. I had been faithful for fourteen years and never so much as looked at another man while Steven was alive. I had always been good, and still I ended up alone. In that moment I chose to believe that I was entitled to grab a slice of happiness wherever I could find it, and that's exactly what I did.

CHAPTER THIRTEEN

IT WAS A couple of days before Valentine's Day, but my developing relationship with Matt had been making the whole month of February bearable. Henry's tenth birthday was in ten days, and I felt a lot of grief about navigating such a big milestone without Steven. As a father, Matt understood that I was excited about Henry reaching double digits but also crushed that his father wasn't alive to celebrate with us. Being able to talk with someone who understood how excruciating this experience was for me really helped.

I was acutely aware that I was now the only keeper of our (my) son's babyhood. I was the only one alive who remembered Henry's actual birth at 2 a.m. I was the one person who could tell him how excited we were to be in a delivery room overlooking Yankee Stadium the day of his birth. I remembered how much my brother and I had delighted in our mother's stories of us as children and how important they were in shaping our core identities.

Rather than dwell on my losses, I thought about my conversation with Matt earlier in the day. Snapchat had the benefit of disappearing chats, but we were able to save the nude photos we shared. There was a playful naughtiness in our communication that I hadn't experienced with anyone before, and I really enjoyed it.

Matt: What are you up to today?

Amy: One of my colleagues is leaving and we're taking her to lunch at a place up by Columbia.

Matt: That sounds like fun.

Amy: Not really. I already see them twice every day for our Zoom staff meetings. Plus, the person leaving is the only other woman in my department. Now it'll just be me and three men.

Matt: You don't like them?

Amy: No, I do like them, two of them are my bosses, but it was just nice having another woman to chat with even if it was virtually.

Matt: Sounds boring. Want to have some fun?

Amy: What did you have in mind?

Matt: Tell me when you get there, and I'll give you some directions to follow.

The restaurant was almost empty that afternoon. The cold weather and reduced on-campus population conspired to keep most people at their desks for lunch. I could see I was the last to arrive as the hostess led me to the large round table my boss had reserved for the occasion. It was big enough to seat double the amount in our party so we could spread out. Everyone was still a bit of a germaphobe at the tail end of the pandemic.

This was my first time seeing my colleagues in person since Steven had died six months ago, but no one hugged me or mentioned my big loss. I felt more isolated than I did during our Zoom meetings. At home I could relax and do other things online while the men dominated the conversation, but here I was stuck in my own invisible bubble.

I took the empty seat between my two bosses and slid my phone onto my lap. We were seated far enough apart that no one could see me in their peripheral vision. There also wasn't anyone sitting directly across from me, so I was practically invisible. I hit send on the message I had already typed in Snapchat:

Amy: I'm here.

Matt: Are you being wholesome?

Amy: No.

Matt: Show me.

I excused myself from the table to go wash my hands in the bathroom and stuck my phone in the back pocket of my jeans. I entered one of the two individual bathrooms, pulled up my sweater and my bra, snapped a selfie, and hit send.

Matt: Good girl.

I washed my hands and went back to the table. It was hard to suppress my grin at the thought of my little secret. Everyone was engrossed in boring work conversation while I just nodded and smiled.

Brunch was being served so I ordered French toast and a glass of red wine. My colleagues had already ordered drinks, so why not?

Just as our orders were being brought to the table my phone vibrated. I flipped it over on my lap under the table and saw a close-up of Matt's cock. Again, I had a difficult time suppressing a smile, especially since I'd already drunk half my wine. Damn, he was so hot.

It was becoming more obvious to me that I had already disconnected from my job. I had worked there for four years and loved supporting independent journalists, but since Steven's death I felt bored and disinterested. While I hated disappointing my boss and colleagues, I felt compelled to escape every part of my old life. They had no idea who I had become after Steven died, and what I had started doing online. I seriously considered taking another leave.

I was in a cab on my way home when I got another message:

Matt: Will you be home around 6 p.m. tonight? I have something for you.

I was secretly thrilled that he was willing to come see me and that he had something for me.

Amy: Aww, that's so nice. I'll be home.

Omg! I was going to meet Matt in person!!

We agreed that after I buzzed him in, I would meet Matt in the little hallway between my front door and the double doors leading out to the street. It was a public space, but still not a high traffic area. What could happen between us anyway? He was just coming over to drop something off.

I could have kept on the clothes I'd worn earlier, but where was the fun in that? I decided to put on the sexy Catholic schoolgirl outfit I'd recently bought. I put it on under a spare three-quarter length bathrobe I had hanging in the small bathroom by the front door.

It was a little after 6 p.m. and I could barely stand still.

Henry was on the couch watching YouTube, not paying me any mind.

"Henry!" I raised my voice, "I have a friend dropping something off for me in a few minutes. I'm going to wait in the hallway." He had his headphones on and was absorbed in a Roblox video game but paused to give me a thumbs up.

Out in the hallway my feet felt cold. I looked down and realized I'd forgotten to put my socks on. I was about to go back into the apartment to get them when I saw Matt outside through the double set of front doors. Each set was made of glass covered in a coarse wrought iron that added more protection than aesthetics.

As I opened the outermost door, the one behind me locked closed. Thank God I had the keys in my robe pocket! For a minute we were face-to-face in the little landing between doors. It was so cold outside that I could feel the cold still clinging to his body.

"Hi, I can only stay for a minute," he said before noticing my feet. "Aren't you cold?"

"Um, yes," I said, turning around to face the innermost door. I was shivering as I grabbed the keys from my pocket and jammed the longest one into the lock and turned.

As I led him a few feet into the warm hallway, he noticed the grand staircase leading to the upper floors. Pointing to the door behind me I said, "I'm in there."

Matt more than met my expectations; there was an instant electricity between us. I felt him devouring me with his warm brown eyes. I opened my robe to reveal my skimpy outfit underneath, and his grin lit me up from the inside. I turned my head toward the first of my two front doors, and he followed me into the windowless space the size of a small closet.

The heavy metal door behind me led into my apartment. The door to the left led down to the basement where the townhouse's owners had storage.

"Nobody lives there," I said, following his gaze, "but we have to be quiet because Henry is right inside."

I said Henry rather than "my son" because in the short time we had been in each other's lives, we had talked a lot about being parents and about our kids. I knew his children's names, ages, and interests, and he knew mine.

I was bouncing on the balls of my feet as we kissed with the frenzied intensity of lovers reunited after months apart. Matt put down the large shopping bag he'd been holding and picked me up as I wrapped my legs around his waist.

Pinned between Matt and the wall, I felt his erection pressing into me through his pants. I knew he wanted me, but did we dare? We were two of a kind, and for better or worse we were going to try.

He put me down and I threw off my robe. I spun around and bent over, putting my hands flat on the floor in front of me. I had kept in relatively good shape and was naturally very flexible. I heard him unzip his pants and then I felt his fingers probe under my short skirt. I realized that Matt wasn't stopping to put on a condom, but I decided it was okay since from what he had told me he wasn't sleeping with anyone else, not even his wife.

He was about to guide himself inside me, when I heard him moan softly. His hands on my waist, his tip pressing on my vulva . . .

"MOM!!!"

We froze.

"MOM!!!"

Fuck, it was Henry.

"I'll be right in," I practically screamed.

I stood up and pulled on my robe as Matt zipped himself back into his pants. He smiled, picked up the shopping bag, and handed it to me.

"I gotta go, but I wanted you to have something for Valentine's Day."

It was still two days away, but I appreciated the gesture more than I could say.

I walked him out to the hallway and watched as he opened the doors out to the street and disappeared into the night.

Back inside my apartment, I opened the bag. There was a giant heart-shaped box of artisanal chocolates and an expensive bottle of red wine. At the bottom, in a clear plastic container, was a buttercream cupcake from the bakery down the block. Matt hadn't forgotten Henry, which meant more than anything he could have given me. Although I knew I was on dicey grounds in terms of my own ethical behavior, I was feeling lonely and so lost. Instead, I chose to focus on the good things about our relationship and left it up to him to worry about the fallout if he got caught.

CHAPTER FOURTEEN

LIFE BEGAN to feel like a series of events I had to "make it through" until the next one came around. It was already mid-February, which meant I had a reprieve until May when I would have to "celebrate" my first Mother's Day without the man who made me a mother.

Work was slow, so I had more free time to spend curating my growing lingerie and sexy costume collection. I wanted to buy more items, but also higher quality pieces. The first luxury lingerie brand that came to mind was La Perla, but $300 for a pair of panties was too steep even for a budding connoisseur like me.

I knew that Lisa occasionally indulged in the finer things, so I texted her for some recommendations. She and my therapist were the only people who knew about my new hobby.

Lisa: Check out Bare Necessities. They always have great sales on a lot of mid and higher end brands. Definitely look at the pearl g-string. I forget who makes it, but you'll know it when you see it.

Bare Necessities sold much more than its name implied. Bracli, a Spanish company, made and marketed the Original Pearl Thong. After I read the description for the double strand pearl panties, I had to have them.

Double strip of pearl necklace with a double function: stimulation of the woman and of both members of the couple in a sexual relationship. The pearl ring must be moved until it touches the clitoris to caress it, and, during penetration, he will have an extra sensation when passing his penis through the hole formed by the two pearl necklaces.

There were so many lingerie brands and styles I decided to begin in the sale section. It didn't make sense to pay full price when I didn't have a good sense of what looked good on me yet. I was high waisted with long legs and a short body (relative to my height) so anything that didn't have adjustable straps would hang too low on my chest.

I discovered what would become one of my favorite lingerie brands in the sale section, although Bluebella was a mid to high end brand. The female led and founded company "champions innovation, inclusivity, and exceptional style above all else, redefining sensuality," and catered to "spirited, fashion-forward women." When I checked out the brand's website, I was intrigued when I saw they had a whole section labeled "provocative." They sold tassels and pasties, harnesses, and quarter coverage bras and bustiers which served to push the breasts up, while leaving the nipple exposed.

For a better selection of naughty costumes, I found the e-retailer 3Wishes. They had a variety of sexy outfits, lingerie, swimwear, and platform heels at different price points. I bought a naughty nurse costume designed as a crotchless bodysuit with red crosses covering the breasts, and a green cheerleader's outfit which had more of a vanilla vibe. Both were so affordable I threw in sexier versions of the Catholic schoolgirl and maid costumes.

I toyed with adding a cheap version of a costume I'd wanted since I was sixteen years old—Princess Leia's copper bikini. At the beginning of *Return of the Jedi,* the third original *Star Wars* movie, Princess Leia is being held captive by Jabba the Hutt as his "slave." She literally has a metal collar around her neck, attached to a chain leash, and is wearing a copper bikini. It was so iconic it even had its own Wikipedia page.

Ultimately, I decided to wait until I found a higher quality costume; plus, I already had plenty of items in my cart. I paid a little extra to have the outfits shipped three-day air (thank you United Parcel Service!). Once all my items arrived, I tried everything on after Henry was asleep.

There was something about cosplay that allowed me to explore my sexuality without shame or self-criticism. The naughty costumes took me out of my reality and lent themselves perfectly to role play, something I hadn't even fantasized about before Steven died. Dressing up allowed me to dissociate from my grieving, heartbroken body and into a space of newness and possibility. I was still managing so much in terms of being a single mom and making sure that Henry was okay. This foray into sexy, adventurous costumes kept me moving forward rather than becoming trapped in the stillness of my weary soul.

Despite my recent experiences with men, I still had not given up hope that a new long-term relationship might be in my future. If I met the "right" man, perhaps I would feel safe to be emotionally available again. Until then, I was going to keep myself occupied with the "potentially right" man.

Feeld was still my dating app of choice, and the place where I connected with Eli. We'd spent a recent morning chatting in my living room and then fucking in my bathroom. He was a nice guy, smart and handsome, but this scenario had become mundane.

I suppose a lot of things felt reductive after my fiery connection with Matt, but there wasn't even a wisp of long-term possibility with him. He was still very much in my life, albeit virtually on Snapchat. And it wasn't just about sex with him; I truly believed that he genuinely cared about me and Henry.

As for Eli, I doubted I would see him again, but this time it would be my choice—and not because I was afraid he would leave me. I just wasn't that into him.

There was no shortage of men who wanted to chat, so I spent a good amount of time doing just that, even if it never led to anything in person. On the flip side, I hadn't experienced matching with a man online and then agreeing to meet the next day to do a sexual role play, until Charley.

We matched a couple of days after I tried on my new costumes. When he told me he was a university professor I immediately thought, *Role play*. Our rapport was easy; we had similar backgrounds growing up in New York, and we both worked in academia, although he was faculty and I was administrative staff.

I probably wouldn't have suggested anything had we worked at the same university, but his school was all the way downtown and mine was uptown so there was no chance we would run into each other on either campus.

Charley was ten years younger than I but seemed older. Not necessarily because he was mature, but because he had established himself as an expert in his field (economics) and was well respected. I wondered if he had fucked any of his graduate assistants, but I found no evidence of misconduct when I verified his identity.

Amy: I know this is cliché, but it could be fun to do a role play, naughty schoolgirl and the professor.

Charley: I've never done a role play before, but it sounds hot.

Amy: It can be very hot. Don't worry, you can just follow my lead.

Charley: Sounds good. I'm free tomorrow.

I hadn't told him about my costume, so when I opened my door the following day dressed in a micromini white tartan skirt, a sleeveless white halter top, and white thigh-high stockings, he was very pleasantly surprised.

I said, "Professor, I'm so grateful you could come over this morning to help me with the extra credit assignment. Please, come in and make yourself comfortable on the couch."

I took his coat, and to his credit, he dove right into his role.

"It's my pleasure to help a promising young student reach their full potential."

"Oh! You think I'm a promising student! Thank you. I promise not to disappoint you, professor."

"I don't think you could disappoint me if you tried, Amy. Now, how can I be of assistance?"

We pretty much stayed in character the whole time. He handed me a condom from his pocket and "instructed" me on how to put it on him, before we continued our sexy role play on my bed.

Charley said, "Amy, you're doing such a good job, I can tell you have been studying very hard."

"Do you really think so, professor? I have been studying nonstop since I started your class. All I ever wanted was to do well so you would notice me."

"I noticed you, Amy."

Charley was fun, but a little too inexperienced. I was more interested in learning rather than teaching at this point in my life, even if I was older than my recent partners by ten to fifteen years. To be honest, I didn't know what I was looking for, but I had more success figuring out what I didn't want rather than finding what I did. In the meantime, I valued new sexual experiences over the possibility of orgasms with strangers.

My preoccupation with the costumes and the apps was helping me get through a long winter. I couldn't believe there were still ten days left in February. I used to hibernate during the winter, only going out and seeing people when I had to. I counted the days until spring and summer. This year I kept myself so busy with men and sex that I barely noticed the cold.

At first, I thought it was just because I'd found a better way to keep warm, but then I realized I hardly ever left my apartment. I told myself it didn't matter, there was nothing good out there for me anyway. It didn't take long for synchronicity to prove me wrong.

CHAPTER FIFTEEN

HENRY HAD recently had a two-week winter break over Christmas and New Year's Day, but apparently that wasn't enough of an inconvenience for parents because now there was something called "mid-winter break." It began on President's Day (the third Monday in February) and lasted through the end of the week.

On the bright side, all these school breaks lit a fire under me to finally hire some help. Jane had started last week, and I could already feel that a weight had been lifted. When Steven died, I'd lost not only my partner, but also the only other adult I trusted 100 percent to take care of Henry in my absence. Of course, no one could take Steven's place when it came to his love for Henry, but having another adult who cared about his welfare was priceless.

Originally from the UK, Jane could have been a real-life Mary Poppins if she'd only had a magic carpet bag. She was in her thirties, with a glorious mane of auburn hair cascading down her back. Jane was smart, funny, patient, and her smile really lit up any room she was in. I felt lucky to have found her. Over time I would come to see that she took care of me almost as much as she cared for Henry.

While I had hired Jane mainly to walk Henry home after school, help him with his homework, and make him dinner before I finished working in my home office at 6 p.m., she was also able to be with him during Mid-Winter Break.

About an hour after Jane arrived that Tuesday, I realized I would need to find another place to work. Henry still came to me whenever he needed something, rendering what little concentration I had left completely useless.

My office at the Journalism School was still being used as a hybrid classroom, so I went out intending to find another quiet place on campus. But it was cold and raining at 10 a.m., and I didn't feel like taking the subway up to Columbia. Instead, I headed for my favorite diner with my laptop, but as I passed the mid-priced hotel across the street an idea popped into my head.

Would it be crazy for me to rent a room to work in for a couple of days?

It wasn't a five-star hotel, but it was a nice place and relatively inexpensive for New York City. I only planned on using the room during the day, so it only made sense if I could check in early.

"Good morning," said the bright-eyed young woman behind the counter. She was wearing a suit jacket over a white blouse, and I wondered if this place was a little fancier than I thought.

"Hello, good morning. Do you have a room available for early check-in today? I'm looking to stay one night, maybe two," I said politely.

"Let me just confirm with housekeeping," she said, reaching for the phone. A few seconds later she said, "Room nine zero nine is available. Will you be staying one night or two?"

"I'll start with one night, thank you."

"Do you need help with your luggage?"

"No thank you," I said, taking the key. I felt a bit strange with only a backpack, but no one gave me a second look.

Room nine zero nine was bigger than I expected. It easily accommodated a king-sized bed, a dresser, and a desk.

It wasn't high end, but the furniture and bedding looked new, and the place was spotless. The bathroom was a little cramped, but it too was clean and had everything I needed.

It was already close to 11 a.m. by the time I was settled and ready to work. I was able to stay on task for half an hour before I felt restless and got up to look out the window with its view over Broadway.

Anxious and lonely, I snapped a selfie with the view behind me and sent it to Matt.

Matt: Ooo, where are you?

Amy: I'm at the hotel across the street from my apartment, working. I didn't feel like going up to campus.

Matt: I'm in the city. Want some company?

Amy: Really? Do you have time?

Matt: Yeah, about thirty minutes. I'll be done with my errand in an hour and then I'll head over to you. What room are you in?

Amy: Nine zero nine.

Matt: Okay, I'll be there around 1 p.m.

I walked into the bathroom and looked at myself in the small mirror hanging over the sink, "Oh. My. God!" I said excitedly to my reflection, "I'm glad you showered and shaved this morning."

I still had an hour until Matt arrived, but there was no way I could concentrate on work now. I was grateful my next Zoom meeting wasn't until 4 p.m.

My stomach grumbled, but I didn't want to eat a big meal. Good thing I'd remembered to throw a couple of granola bars into my backpack. I walked out of the bathroom and found my backpack on the bed. I rifled through it, easily finding a granola bar, but I also saw some white lacy fabric.

"What is that?" I said, tugging on the material. Once I had pulled the whole thing out, I saw it was my new sexy maid's costume. Not the one I'd worn for Joel; this one was skimpier.

I'd taken some photos of myself wearing it a couple of days ago, but how had it gotten into my backpack? I closed my eyes to think and saw a vision of myself grabbing the costume off the hook this morning right before I left the apartment.

My eyes snapped open, and I could feel my heart racing.

"I planned this?" I said out loud.

I couldn't have known there would be an available room, let alone predict that Matt would be able to meet me. On some level I knew that if (or when) we connected again in the flesh it wouldn't be planned. His schedule wasn't flexible (neither was his marital status), so he'd have to fit me in whenever he could. It just so happened he had an opening the third week in February at the same time I had a hotel room and a naughty maid's costume.

I felt both exhilarated and scared. There was such deep intimacy between us online, I knew every inch of his body intimately in two dimensions, but in three dimensions he was still a stranger. What would he feel like on top of me? How would he taste? How would his gaze make me feel?

It was just after 1 p.m. when I heard the door to room nine zero nine open behind me, followed by the gentle click indicating the lock had been engaged. I had specifically left it open a crack so Matt wouldn't have to knock, thus ruining the surprise of catching the "maid" tidying the room.

Before he uttered a word, I spun around to face him and said, "Oh, sir! You surprised me!" Mock flustered, I continued, "I just finished making up your room. Is there anything else you need before I go?"

Matt's grin and knowing look told me he understood the role he was meant to play. "As a matter of fact," he said, crossing the distance between us in two strides, "I'm glad you asked."

He took my hand and pressed it firmly against his crotch. I could feel his erection throbbing through his pants, and he said, "I've had a very hard day."

I began to run my hand along the outline of his shaft and asked, "Is this helping, sir?"

"Mmmm, yes," he said, "but I think I'd be more comfortable with my pants off."

"Of course, sir," I said, reaching for his belt buckle. "Let me do that for you."

I worked efficiently, but without rushing, to unbuckle his belt. After unbuttoning and unzipping, I got on my knees to pull his pants and boxers down before taking him in my mouth. He moaned.

I stopped what I was doing and looked up to ask, "Is this helping, sir?"

Matt pulled me to my feet, picked me up in his arms, and gently tossed me onto the bed. I watched as he took off his shirt and shoes, then stepped out of his pants.

I moved to take my arms out of the top of my costume, but he said, "No, leave it on."

"Yes sir," I said, dropping my arms back down to my sides.

"Come lie down on your stomach in front of me," he said neutrally.

I must have looked skeptical because he continued, "I'm going to hold you upside down while I devour you."

That didn't sound bad at all.

I scooted down toward him on my belly, and he put his hands on my waist and lifted. I used my arms to push myself up into a handstand as he wrapped his arms around me and then took a step back. Suddenly, I was dangling upside down, face pressed between his legs in what I could only describe as a vertical sixty-nine position.

I took Matt in my mouth again as he pulled my g-string to the side with his teeth. I felt his warm breath on me as his tongue probed the most intimate folds of my flesh. The blood rushing to my head, I felt my temples pulsing to the rhythm of my own heartbeat.

We probably stayed like that for ten minutes, and just as I was beginning to feel woozy, he stepped back in front of the bed. I reached out my arms, resting my palms on the duvet as he pushed me into a somersault. I tucked my head and rolled, landing on my back, breathless.

He lay down next to me and we laughed and kissed, and then he was on top of me, thrusting like a piston. I wrapped my legs around his waist, squeezing as I orgasmed and pulled him in deeper until he exploded inside me.

I knew from our first encounter that he hadn't planned to wear a condom. Like a lot of men, he said they lessened his sensitivity and pleasure. I normally wouldn't have accepted that as an excuse, but I wasn't worried about him sleeping with multiple partners, and he hadn't expressed concern about my recent sexual history. In retrospect maybe I should have been more careful, but I really trusted him.

We lay there, holding each other for a few minutes, each of us trying to catch our breath.

I knew he had to go. I pushed him up and cleaned myself with some tissues as he showered. I found a bathrobe in the coat closet and wrapped myself in it as Matt dried himself with a towel.

He dressed quickly, gave me one last kiss, and opened the door before disappearing down the hallway. I took a quick survey of the room: the bed was slightly rumpled, but everything else was undisturbed.

At 5:30 p.m. I gathered my things and packed up to go home. I felt lonely. It wasn't easy for me to separate the closeness we had just shared from more tender feelings of . . . love? I didn't want to love him, but with loneliness came grief, and my grief carried all the love I had for Steven with no place to go. It felt so easy to conflate intimacy with genuine love.

As the door to room nine zero nine closed behind me, I felt a sense of loss, like I had just been left again. I got in the elevator and pulled out my phone to check Feeld. Just as the doors opened into the lobby, I saw I had a new match.

I'll look at it later, I told myself, *after Henry goes to bed.* Knowing I had a new match didn't alleviate my loneliness entirely, but it gave me something to look forward to. As I pushed through the hotel's revolving door and out into the blustery darkness, I was unaware of the turn my life was about to take.

CHAPTER SIXTEEN

FEBRUARY melted into March, and it felt like spring was just around the corner. It would have been easy to believe the worst of winter was over, but I still had memories of April snowstorms from when I was a kid. I would not be lulled into a false sense of weather security.

I was in a good mood, though, because there was a new man on the horizon. It was the guy I'd matched with on my way out of the hotel, but I hadn't decided how I felt about him yet. His name was Marco; he was divorced with a daughter the same age as my son.

Honestly, I was surprised that I had even "liked" him in the first place. Before we started chatting, I checked out his profile to refresh my memory, and the only information was his name and height, six feet two inches. I was puzzled until I looked through all his photos and saw how hot he was.

Marco was a completely different type of gorgeous than Matt. I likened Matt to a golden god, chiseled to perfection from Carrara marble by the expert hand of a Renaissance sculptor. Marco, on the other hand, was all about what was going on above the neck.

He had a full head of shiny jet-black hair, thick and wavy, to the point of loose curls. In one photo a lock had fallen forward onto his forehead, and I imagined reaching up to push it back into place like Barbra Streisand's Katie in the 1970s movie *The Way We Were*.

His body was not cut like Matt's (whose is?), but he looked like he kept in shape. Marco's smile was magnetic, and that was just in the photos. I wondered what it would feel like to have that smile looking down at me in real life. If he was being truthful about his height, I was a whole foot shorter than he was.

We messaged for a bit on the app, and I told him I was a widow and a mom.

Marco: How is your son doing? I imagine it was very difficult losing his father.

Amy: He's doing well. His school is very supportive, which is so helpful. I'm the one who is overwhelmed.

Marco: Of course. It must be quite an adjustment.

Amy: My life is completely different, but I wouldn't say I've adjusted.

Our conversation was vanilla, more like something I would expect on Bumble rather than Feeld. Maybe he was just normal while Matt and I were degenerate sex fiends.

Was I looking for "normal," though? I thought he might loosen up off the app, so I messaged him my mobile number. Almost immediately my phone vibrated with his incoming text: Hi, it's Marco.

I'd learned my lesson with Matt, so before I responded, I ran his number through a verification website. He was exactly who he said he was, and was even truthful about his age, early forties. I made a note of his birthday, which was a week before mine, and I thought, *July has always been my favorite month.*

It was nice having two men who cared about me, especially because they didn't ask for more than I had already offered. I even told them about each other, which I thought would be weird, but it wasn't. I had never had relationships like this, although now the term I heard all the time was "situationship."

Speaking of situations, I took another leave from work, through June. I wished I knew how to make myself care about my job like I did before Steven died. I felt like a switch was flipped off and I didn't know how to turn it back on. I was beginning to think I didn't want to flip it. I didn't want to go back to that old life where I was constantly reminded that Steven had died.

I may have felt disoriented having created this new life in such a short amount of time, but no one in this life knew Steven. No one was here to remind me that they missed him, too.

"Okay Amy," I said to myself in the mirror. "This may not be the life you planned, but you're going to make the most of it."

Marco and I were finally going to meet in person two weeks after we matched on Feeld. I still felt ambivalent about him; he lived so far away, and he was a little uptight. More specifically, the way he expressed himself verbally and in writing felt "wordy." I knew that deep down I was already preparing myself for disappointment, which felt safer than liking him, opening my heart, and then being left again. A previous conversation went like this:

Marco: I'm going to be in your neighborhood later today visiting one of my cousins.

Amy: Oh, did you want to try and get together?

Marco: I won't have time, but I was eager to tell you due to the proximity.

Huh?

He had loosened up, although we hadn't met that time, but I got the feeling he never really let his guard down. He would never send me, or anyone else, a dick pic. Maybe he was just a serious person in general. In any case, I was about to find out.

I wasn't sure how things would go today, so I hedged my bets by wearing a lacy pink bodysuit under jeans and a T-shirt. The top was more like a harness since it didn't have bra panels. The bottom was crotchless, but I forgot there was a large taffeta bow that tied in the back. I was trying to jam the bow into the top of my jeans when the buzzer rang.

"Shit," I said out loud as I ran down the hall to buzz Marco in.

Bang! Bang! The double set of front doors slammed shut and I knew he'd made it into the hallway. I was only able to get the loops of the bow into my waistband, so it must have looked like I had two long pink tails from the back.

I'll just keep him in front of me for now, I thought to myself while I opened the thick metal door in front of me. Every time I stepped into the little windowless landing between doors I thought about Matt.

Stop it Amy, focus, I told myself as I opened the door into the public hallway and . . . he was right there, in front of me, arm outstretched, knuckles poised to knock.

I stood there frozen for a couple of seconds gazing up at him. He looked exactly like his photos. As he lowered his arm I saw it, that grin, looking down at me. I felt seen and wanted in a way I hadn't since Steven died, and I felt lucky to be the object of his attention, and perhaps affection.

"Hi!" I said a little too enthusiastically.

"Hi. Can I come in?" he asked shyly.

"Oh! Yes, of course," I said, stepping to the side to let him pass.

He walked into the living room/kitchen, and I closed the doors behind him.

"Can I take your coat?" I said, arm outstretched, ready to take it from him.

Amy, get a hold of yourself. You aren't wearing the maid's costume. I was glad I had real clothes on because I felt a little exposed as it was. I really thought he would be shorter or not as good-looking in person, but Marco looked taller than six feet two inches and was even more handsome in the flesh.

"Please, sit down," I said motioning to the small couch. "Can I get you some water?"

"Yes, water would be great," he said as he took a seat on the larger couch.

I took a few steps over to the large Sub-Zero refrigerator, which was paneled with the same wood used for the cabinets. If I ever had enough money to buy a Sub-Zero, I would leave it uncovered, its shiny silver on full display, but that was my landlord for you. I'd already filled glasses with ice water for both of us in anticipation of getting hot and sweaty. I was a good hostess, and it made sense to hydrate.

I handed him his water and he took a sip before putting it on the coffee table in front of him. I sat on the shag rug across from him on the other side of the table.

We fell easily into a conversation about our work and our kids. I learned more about his childhood; like Joel he'd been shaped by familial infidelity. He also had older siblings closer to my age, so we shared many of the same cultural references from the 1980s even though he was twelve years my junior.

The hours melted away and by the time I looked at the time it was almost noon. At this point I wasn't even sure we were going to get naked. Had we already moved into the friend zone?

CHAPTER SEVENTEEN

MARCO MUST have noticed me looking at my phone because he asked, "Hey, what time is it?"

"Oh, it's noon." I answered.

Rising from the couch, he flashed that shy grin again. He walked around to my side of the coffee table, and I thought he was going to ask me where the bathroom was—but he didn't.

Instead, he extended a hand down to me, indicating he wanted me to stand. My hand looked tiny in his, and I felt his strength as he lifted me to my feet. Still holding hands, he slowly spun me around and asked, "What's this?" as he gave one end of my pink bow "tails" a tug.

Marco didn't pull hard enough to move me back, but I took a step toward him anyway.

"Why don't you see for yourself," I said as I lifted my arms so he could take my shirt off.

He lifted my shirt up, turning it inside out as it cleared my head. He dropped it on the coffee table, and I smiled as I slowly turned to face him. *Won't he be surprised to see me bare breasted,* I thought.

Cocking an eyebrow, he leaned down to kiss me. It was slow and tentative, probing for my consent to go further. I pressed my lips more firmly against his while my tongue explored his mouth. I felt his large hands cupping my breasts, then pinching my erect nipples.

I reached for the waistband of his jeans and pulled him closer before moving to unbutton and unzip them. I took my lips off his and we locked eyes in silent agreement to move deeper into each other.

Pushing his jeans and boxers down, I sank to my knees. Every part of him was beautiful, natural, and untouched by a razor or clippers. A size queen, someone who prefers large penises (saw it on Feeld and had to Google it), may have been disappointed, but I wasn't.

Confident I could give him a uniquely pleasurable experience, I took all of him in my mouth, working my tongue and lips until he filled me completely. His deep moan reverberated throughout my body, and I knew I had achieved the desired effect.

As women we learn that a man's penis is his most prized asset, but also his Achilles heel. To speak words less than rapturous praise and gratitude is a blasphemy capable of crushing his self-esteem. We know to tread oh-so-lightly, for even a neutral word, if misconstrued, can reduce him to a shell of his former self. In general, and if you want him to satisfy you, it is best to worship at his altar and pledge undying devotion.

The truth though, was that we did compare lovers; at least I did. I didn't rank by size, but by how the whole man made me feel. It wasn't just about what was in his shorts, but most men wouldn't believe me.

Marco was unapologetically himself, and while I appreciated his confidence, I also wanted to be pursued. Why shouldn't men act like peacocks? I love to see them performing on par with those magnificent tail feathers, shaking them to attract mates. Seduction is an art form, and I like to know my partner is putting in some effort too.

I was getting a subtle vibe from him, "You get what you see, take it or leave it," which was decidedly not peacock energy, but he was so fucking sexy that I let it go. I liked what I saw, and I was going to take it.

I looked up to see his arm extended, his hand ready to take mine again. I let him help me to my feet, watching as he kicked his shoes off. His pants and boxers already around his ankles, he stepped out of them easily.

We were still holding hands as I led him down the long hallway to my bedroom. We had another hour before he had to leave, and I was determined to make the most of it.

When we entered the bedroom, I still had my jeans on, while Marco was naked below the waist.

"We're a little mismatched," I said, looking down at my legs.

"What should we do about that?" he said, smiling.

I unbuttoned my jeans and pulled the zipper down.

"I need help," I said, letting my arms fall to my sides.

"Oh, do you?" he said, taking a step closer so we were almost touching.

Marco took my hand and led me over to the bed.

I took in the large tufted headboard and blue flowered comforter as if for the first time. They were more feminine than my usual aesthetic. I remembered wanting to make my room feel more womanly, warm, and inviting. I hoped it would soften me after so much time being strong for everyone else.

I lay down on my back and lifted my ass as Marco grabbed the hem of each pant leg and pulled them off. He dropped my jeans on the floor, pulled off his shirt, and then lay down next to me.

We turned on our sides, facing each other, and started kissing. He reached down to explore the exposed area between my legs with his free hand, easily finding my most sensitive spot. He applied pressure and began to rub, but no man has ever gotten it exactly right the first time.

I knew we didn't have all day, so I said, "Hold on for a sec, let me get Lulu."

He looked intrigued as I ran into my bathroom and opened the bottom drawer of my vanity. I pulled out Lulu, my vibrator, about the size and shape of a handheld microphone. After my experience with Joel, I knew I wanted something with a smaller profile and a rechargeable battery.

I walked over to my bedside table and got a pump full of lube.

"You named your vibrator Lulu?" Marco said, chuckling.

"Haha, no. That's the brand name," I said, handing him the lube-covered vibrator.

He took it from me, and I pointed to the camouflaged on/off button before laying down on my back, knees bent and spread apart. He put Lulu against my bare skin and turned her on. I could tell this wasn't his first time holding a vibrator as I rocked my hips back and forth.

It didn't take long for me to climax, shaking not just my legs but my whole body. I felt safe with him, and I just let myself relax knowing that he could take care of me. As I caught my breath, Marco reached over and put Lulu on my bedside table. He leaned over to kiss me, and I reached my hand down to feel his hardness.

This was usually the moment when a man grabbed a condom from the back pocket of his jeans, but Marco's pants were in the living room.

"I don't have any condoms . . ." I said, hoping this prompted him to retrieve whatever he brought.

Instead, he answered, "I'm not currently sleeping with anyone, and I just got tested."

I sat up. This was going to require more of a conversation than I anticipated.

"I'm using condoms with other guys, but not with one married man," I offered even though he hadn't asked.

"If I start sleeping with other women I will use condoms too."

"Okay."

Had Marco not worked in the healthcare industry I probably wouldn't have believed him. I knew it was still stupid to take him at his word anyway, but maybe on some level I was continuing to choose risky behavior as penance for not saving Steven.

We resumed where we left off and he moved to get on top of me as I lifted my legs, resting one on each of his shoulders.

"I'm very flexible," I told him.

He leaned down, bracing himself on one arm while using the other to guide himself inside me. With both arms on either side of my head now, he was so close I could feel his pelvis rock against me with every thrust.

Marco bent his elbows as if doing a pushup and I was almost bent in half. It felt a little weird to have the tops of my thighs hovering so close to my chest, but the closeness we achieved was intense. Bracing my bent knees on each of his shoulders, I was able to lift my pelvis up to meet his.

He was not an overly verbal lover, but this man knew how to fuck. That was the only word that came to mind, and I wondered for a second if I had lost all inhibitions. I supposed it didn't really matter what I called it; we were both consenting adults.

"Yes, baby, yes," I said, looking up at him.

He thrusted harder, before exploding for the second time. We lay on our backs for a minute, disheveled and sweaty.

"Can I take a quick shower?" he asked.

"Of course," I said, jumping up. "I'll turn it on for you."

I walked past him, and he followed me into my bathroom. This room "sold," or in my case "rented," the apartment as far as I was concerned.

Everything was custom from the marble vanities to the miniature white subway tiles covering the walls. The shower had a marble bench where I sat to shave, and the shower fixture shot out water like hard rain massaging my skin. It was a full mind/body experience.

I opened the glass door and turned on the water.

"Nice," Marco said, moving past me to get underneath.

I leaned in to show him how to adjust the temperature and then closed the glass behind him. It was almost immediately fogged by steam, but I stood there watching him anyway. A feeling of safety washed over me, and for a minute I didn't feel so alone in the world.

Marco turned off the water, and the feeling washed out like the tide. I put on my fluffy white bathrobe and handed him a towel when he opened the shower door. While he dried off, I walked back into the bedroom, picked our clothes up from the floor, and put his shirt on the bed.

"I'll meet you in the living room. I'm going to get some water," I said loud enough so he would hear me.

I made my way down the hallway to the kitchen and refilled our glasses with cold water. Marco must have been right on my heels because when I turned around, he was pulling up his jeans. After he zipped and buttoned himself up, I handed him the glass of water and he drank most of it in one gulp.

"It's good to rehydrate," I told him, smiling.

"Yes, it is," he said, stepping into his shoes and bending over to tie them.

He followed me toward the door, and I grabbed his coat from the closet. As he put it on, I opened the thick metal door. He stopped in the little windowless landing and kissed me.

"I had a really good time," he told me.

"I did too," I said.

"I'll see you soon," he said as he opened the other door into the public hallway.

I watched as he moved through the double sets of doors and out into the real world.

It would be lovely if Marco was the first (unmarried) man to want to see me twice, I thought. I wanted to believe him, that he would see me soon, but I was too scared of being hurt. The level of pain I felt after Joel discarded me was too high a price, and I couldn't afford to pay it again. Lucky for me, I still had the apps.

CHAPTER EIGHTEEN

SPRING MADE a hasty retreat at the beginning of April, but my allergies were already in full swing. I was fine if I remembered to take my antihistamine and stay in the apartment most of the day.

Marco and I had been keeping in touch texting, sexting, and on one occasion, phone sexing. I wanted to sleep with him again, and see where it might lead, but I was afraid that if I expressed too much interest he would run in the other direction like Joel and Ed.

I felt so happy when he texted me:

Marco: So, when am I going to see you again?

Amy: I think that's up to you, Marco.

He'd told me multiple times about how busy he was with work and his daughter, while I was on leave from my job until June. Since he had a car, it made more sense for him to drive into Manhattan. Still, I didn't want to appear overly eager and text back, *Any time, I'm always available!*

Marco: What do you mean?

Amy: My schedule is flexible, like my body. When are you available?

Marco: Oh, okay. How about Wednesday? I can be at your place by 10:30 a.m.

Amy: Great. See you then.

I would not allow myself to get overly excited about seeing him for a second time, especially since that hadn't happened with anyone else. I also didn't want to set myself up to be let down, again.

In the meantime, I kept myself busy with something special I had lined up with Matt, who would be coming by later that day. A few weeks earlier I'd found a custom version of the Princess Leia costume I'd been looking for on Etsy and texted the link to Lisa.

Amy: Look what I just bought!!

Lisa: OMG! That's amazing!

Amy: I know, right?! It feels like a million years ago we saw *Return of the Jedi* in the theater! We must have been about sixteen!

Lisa: Wow, where did the time go?

The costume had arrived a few days ago and I'd already done an amazing photoshoot using my new tripod with a ring light and a Bluetooth remote for my iPhone camera.

I was thrilled with the results as I was able to capture shots from overhead while lying in my empty bathtub. I felt beautiful and confident, like a real model, but I took the most pride in my skills as a photographer.

In my mind, what I was doing was much more than just taking pictures. I also did my hair and makeup and paid careful attention to the lighting and positioning of my body. The aesthetic I created was uniquely mine, and both the process and the product brought joy into my life. Rather than feeling sad and alone as I had so much of the time, I was able to alchemize those emotions to use in my creative projects.

The buzzer rang, and I ran to hit the intercom, unlocking the two front doors. My heart was pounding, but not from my sprint down the hallway. There was something about Matt that both excited and scared me. He was a wildcard, all urges and impulsivity.

In caveman times, he would have been the one to volunteer for dangerous missions, like getting past a tiger to hunt and gather. When told there was a fifty-fifty chance of survival, he would confidently say, "I'll take those odds," just before he was disemboweled.

I was sure he wouldn't hurt me on purpose, but I wondered if he always had control of his strength. To be safe I had started giving my therapist the full names and cell numbers of all the men I spent time with in real life.

The telltale *bang bang* of the two front doors closing told me he'd made it into the building. I'd told Matt I had a surprise for him, but I didn't give him any clues. I wondered if he was too young to recognize my costume. He had only been five years old when the movie came out.

I felt my pulse throb through a vein in my neck as I swung open the thick metal door and . . . he was right there, standing in front of me, all five foot nine inches, 195 pounds of him. He must have been 85 percent muscle, or more.

He took a step back, his eyes locking with mine before letting them drop to my breasts, stomach, and the exposed space between the two fabric panels of my costume.

His lips parted into a wide grin, and he chuckled, "Princess Leia in the copper bikini! Every boy's fantasy when I was a kid!"

I did a little twirl, and the fabric panels covering my legs billowed out, revealing my nakedness. I was so happy he recognized the costume that I took a little bow before pulling him into my apartment by the waistband of his jeans.

We started kissing slowly, but when I started to speed things up, pushing my lips more firmly on his, he pulled back to whisper in my ear, "We have two hours, let's take it a little slower."

"Yes," was all I could manage to say.

"I want you to worship me," he said, grabbing the outline of his hard shaft pressing against the inside of his pants.

His smiling eyes told me he was in character.

Bowing my head I said, "Of course."

Matt put one hand under my chin, gently guiding it up so our eyes met. His other hand reached out for mine, and I gladly gave it to him as he led me over to the small couch.

Standing face-to-face, I reached down to deftly unbutton his jeans, pulling them down with his boxers. As his erection sprung free, escaping its close confines, he sat down. I kneeled in front of him, my bare knees cushioned by the plush shag rug covering the living room floor.

Before I could start "worshiping" him, Matt broke character, leaned forward, and said, "Hey, where's your phone? Let's take some video!"

We had traded many naked photos of ourselves, but we hadn't shot any video together.

I held my phone, arm outstretched toward him.

"Let's do it!" I said, as we both grinned ear-to-ear, quite unlike the characters we pretended to be.

Later that night, when I was alone in my bedroom, I replayed the last clip we recorded. It was taken with the phone on my bedside table, rather than Matt holding it. It was a side view of him banging me quite aggressively from behind. I was on all fours on the bed in my Princess Leia costume; Matt was standing behind me, his feet on the floor, naked. Neither of our faces were visible, although we did call out each other's names (duh!).

I was critical of my appearance rather than my performance. The first thing I noticed was how jiggly my thigh was (it was a side view so only one was visible), but once I got past that, I could see that the video was steamy.

It was late, but I put off going to sleep. The loneliness when I went to bed each night was overwhelming. I just wanted to sleep next to a man for one night, to feel the sturdiness and safety I once had. Even the distraction of my costumes, the apps, and now the video could not completely take away my desire for some real connection.

I wasn't ready for a man to stay overnight in my apartment, but renting a hotel room felt doable, and I began to plan out a way to make that happen. I was nervous because I hadn't spent a night away from my son in at least four years. Steven's death had exacerbated Henry's anxiety, causing him to worry about something happening to me when we weren't together. Planning a getaway, even for just one night, hadn't been easy. Henry was comfortable with Jane, so I was relieved when I texted her and she confirmed she could stay over with him one night the following week. I knew it was something we both needed, but I agreed to a short Facetime at 8 p.m. to say good night.

When I reserved a one-bedroom suite at the Park Hyatt on 57th Street I still hadn't decided who I was going to invite to stay over with me. I knew who I wanted, but the thought of asking Marco made me feel uncomfortably vulnerable. I wouldn't be crushed if he said no, but I knew I would be disappointed. As it turned out, he said yes. I was so thrilled that I also booked a couples massage for us in the hotel spa the next morning.

CHAPTER NINETEEN

A WEEK LATER I was in the hotel elevator waiting for it to take me up to the twentieth floor. I stood there for a good two minutes before I realized I wasn't moving. I pressed my floor again, but it wouldn't light up. Frustrated, I was about to head back to reception when someone else got in. I watched as they held their keycard up to what I now realized was a little sensor before tapping the button for the eighteenth floor.

I casually stepped forward and repeated the stranger's actions with my own keycard and pressed twenty. This time the numbers lit up, signaling the elevator would stop on my floor. I may be a native New Yorker, but I had never stayed at a five-star hotel in the city before.

Now that my desire to sleep next to a man was about to be fulfilled, I realized there was more to it. I didn't just want to "sleep" next to a man, I wanted to have wild crazy sex with him and then fall asleep exhausted in his arms. Was that too much to wish for?

I had never done anything like this with Steven, which added a layer of guilt I hadn't been expecting. Why hadn't we treated ourselves? After Henry was born, we never went away, just the two of us. When you have your first (and only) baby at forty-four years old, the extended family babysitting pool has already been drained dry.

Plus, from the time he was a baby, Henry had separation anxiety. It was just easier for the three of us to go away as a family than leave him with Steven's parents. I was also a nervous first-time mother and couldn't imagine leaving my baby with anyone for more than a few hours.

I finally made it to the twentieth floor and found my room at the end of the long hallway. Pressing my keycard against the sensor I heard the click of the lock followed by a pulsing green light indicating the door was unlocked.

As I turned the handle and swung open the door, I saw floor to ceiling windows overlooking the New York skyline. I walked into the living area, which felt industrial and masculine, all dark woods and brown leather. The vibe was business over romance, which I supposed fit the occasion.

It had taken me longer than I expected to check in and get up to the room, so it was already 5 p.m. when I finally kicked off my shoes and turned on the TV. Marco was working late so he wouldn't be here for a few more hours. I texted that I'd left a keycard for him at reception so he wouldn't have to knock on the door.

I was a bit antsy, so I took a bath in the large soaking tub. Even though I had a tub like that in my apartment, it still felt special and decadent. I dropped in a few of the fizzy bath tablets and soaked for twenty minutes, allowing the hot water to gently loosen and massage my tight muscles. It was never easy for me to relax. Even though I was the one who wanted some time away from Henry, it didn't mean it wasn't also stressful.

Jane was a huge help, but I was still a solo parent, and there was so much for me to manage. Although my grief always got pushed away, my loneliness was constant.

The silence felt heavenly as I lay on the bed warm and cozy in the hotel's thick cotton bathrobe. I was thinking about pouring a glass of wine from a bottle in the minibar when I got a text from Marco. He was on his way and would arrive in twenty minutes!

I was wearing nothing but the pearl g-string under my robe. I pulled the robe tightly around my neck in preparation for my call with Henry. I had my laptop, so I called from my computer; he answered on the second ring and my screen immediately filled with his big toothy grin.

How was it possible to love someone so much and still be so grateful to be away from them?

"Mom, when are you coming home?"

"Tomorrow, honey, in the afternoon," I said for the twentieth time.

Just then, the door opened, and Marco casually walked in. He saw I was on a call with Henry and went to check out the rest of the suite while I carefully tried to extricate myself from the conversation.

"Okay sweetie, I've got to go now. I love you so much, and I can't wait to see you when you get home from school tomorrow!"

"I miss you. Why can't you come home now?"

"Because I'm coming home tomorrow. I am so proud of you. I know this is hard . . ."

I heard Jane in the background calling Henry to have a little snack before bed. Desperate times, desperate measures.

"Okay, bye Mom," he said while simultaneously closing his laptop.

Finally, it's grown-up time, I thought.

I found Marco lounging on the king-sized bed, still fully clothed, clicking through channels on the large flat-screen TV.

"Everything okay with Henry?" he asked, clicking the TV off.

"Yeah, he's fine," I said, ready to change the subject. "Did you eat dinner, babe?"

"No, I came straight here after work. Are you hungry?" he asked, flashing me that smile.

"Very hungry," I said as I opened my robe. I let it slide slowly off my body and onto the floor.

"Come here," he said, extending his hand to me.

He looked so good, sitting there on the edge of the bed. I felt lucky to have him with me for the night. As much as I appreciated being more independent in my new life, sometimes I could feel the loneliness creeping in. I often felt alone, even when I was with people, but I avoided attachment anyway because for me, love and loss were forever intertwined. If that meant avoiding the former to prevent the latter, that's what it had to be.

We had such a great night that we barely made it on time for our couples massage the next morning.

"Should I leave my boxers on?" Marco asked, as we quickly undressed.

"I think so," I said, uncertain. "I'm leaving my crotchless panties on."

"What if they notice, what will they think?" he said, mock scandalized.

"That you're the luckiest man alive," I said, laughing.

We left our clothes on an empty shelf and quickly dashed under the warm blankets covering each massage table. Lying face down as instructed, the two masseuses entered the room and dimmed the lights.

I closed my eyes, surrendering my other senses to the room's delights: a light citrusy scent filled my nostrils, while strong hands kneaded and rubbed the knots out of my back and shoulders. I heard Marco's breath slowing and deepening as the calm Zen music played quietly in the background.

I didn't want to fall asleep and miss a minute of this experience, but the atmosphere conspired against me. Despite my best efforts, I felt myself drifting away on a soft fluffy cloud of my own contentment.

Of course, it made sense that we both fell asleep since we didn't get much of it the night before. After our quickie on the bed, we'd ordered room service: fresh spaghetti covered in a thick, rich Bolognese sauce, a loaf of crusty bread, and a bottle of Chilean Pinot Noir.

We spent the rest of the night having sex in a variety of positions, and on every piece of furniture in the suite. It was 2 a.m. by the time we made it back to the bed, where Marco promptly rolled onto his side and fell into a deep sleep. I stayed up for a little while watching his back rise and fall with each breath.

I longed to curl myself around him, to feel anchored by the solidness of his body next to mine, but I didn't dare. Joel, the first man I was with after Steven died, had reminded me that men do not like clingy women, so I vowed to keep my needs to myself.

We woke a few hours later and fucked in the steam shower until breakfast arrived; I didn't think I ever felt so dirty and so clean at the same time. We wolfed down some toast and coffee before heading to the rooftop pool and spa for our massages.

I felt a light rubbing sensation on the side of my arm and opened my eyes.

"How was that?" I heard Marco's masseuse ask.

His voice groggy with sleep, he said, "That was wonderful, thank you."

"Please feel free to stay in the common areas of the spa or by the pool for as long as you want. There are robes in the closet and two glasses of champagne right over here on the counter," my masseuse said, pointing to two flutes filled with crisp bubbly.

Marco and I could not stop grinning at each other as the two masseuses stepped out of the room, the door closing softly behind them.

"That was really amazing, thank you Amy," he said earnestly.

"Thank you for sharing this experience with me," I said, grabbing two robes from the closet and handing him one.

We wrapped ourselves in soft cotton, and then Marco handed me a glass of champagne.

"Do you want to hang out by the pool for a little while before we head out?" he asked.

"Sounds great," I said, clinking my glass with his.

The indoor pool deck was empty; it had been unseasonably cold for April in New York, so we easily grabbed a couple of lounge chairs. As we continued drinking champagne in our fancy robes Marco said, “Let’s take a picture.”

I felt like I was about to burst with happiness. I wanted a photo to remember the moment when I felt real joy again, but I was too scared to ask for one. I worried he would think I was being possessive if I asked for a picture of us together.

Marco had made it clear from the moment we met that he was not looking for anything serious or exclusive, but I assumed after our condom conversation that he would mention if he was seeing other women. Since he hadn’t said anything about it, I felt confident that he was only sleeping with me. Still, I didn’t want to scare him away.

And deep down I wasn’t sure what I wanted from him. Part of me longed to get back the safety and security I’d had with my husband by jumping into another relationship, but I also wanted to avoid that type of love—and potential loss—at all costs.

Marco held his phone at arm’s length to snap a selfie. We were both a little disheveled and bleary eyed from the massage and lack of sleep, but I was grinning like the Cheshire Cat. My eyes twinkled back at me, and in that moment, I thought it might be worth opening myself up to love, and possible loss again, if I could look and feel like that more often.

CHAPTER TWENTY

THE FOLLOWING week Lisa was back in town visiting her mother for Easter, and I invited her to come over for an afternoon cocktail. One of the new things I had decided widowed Amy needed was a fully stocked bar. It was more of an aesthetic, a sign of sophistication and worldliness. In my old life with Steven, we occasionally had a bottle of red wine with dinner, but that was it.

I still didn't drink a lot, but I enjoyed champagne with Marco. A martini every now and then was good too. I found a great oval-shaped cart with two mirrored shelves on Wayfair and ordered a home bar starter kit from a local wine shop.

"I think I understand what's going on with me and men," I said, dropping a fistful of ice cubes into the shaker.

"You're lonely. There's nothing wrong with that," Lisa said.

"Yes, that's true, but I'm noticing a pattern." I poured gin into the shaker and continued, "Every time I'm in a relationship and in love, there's hardly any sex, but once I'm out of the relationship all I want is sex. It's like the two can't go together, sex and a relationship."

Lisa pierced a third briny olive onto a toothpick. "Yeah, I guess I see what you mean. Isn't that what happened with Rob?"

I measured the vermouth and said, "Yes. Hardly any sex during the three years we lived together, but after I broke up with him, I cashed out my 401(k), moved to Paris, and fucked a bunch of hot firemen."

That adventure began over twenty years ago, in the summer of 1999, when I was in my early thirties. My mother saw my breakup as an opportunity for us to travel together again so she booked a three-week trip to Paris and Nice.

We did the regular touristy things, but I also looked at *Time Out* Magazine for special events related to Bastille Day celebrations (France's Independence Day) and found out that every July, firemen's balls became hot spots at fire stations across Paris, as well as the rest of France.

One night my mother and I found a party nearby, but she was tired and left early. I stayed to chat with a very handsome fireman named Jacques and ended up having sex with him at 3 a.m. back at his fire station, a barge on the Seine River off the Quai de Conti, with a perfect view of Pont Neuf and the Northwestern tip of Île de la Cité.

The French firemen did like their gatherings and had many on the barge. I became friends with some of the other girlfriends and ended up staying in Paris for seven months after my mother went back to the United States. Parties at night, sightseeing during the day; it was a fun time in my life, but eventually I moved home, got a job, and became a responsible person again.

I met Steven a few years later and thus began my responsible but less sexy cycle of life, which lasted for fourteen years. It ended when he died, and I was still trying to figure out how to create a new life for myself and for Henry. Everything was different now. I was a responsible mother, so I made sure that I kept my son separate from the new part of my life that involved men. I had been sure I wasn't ready for another serious relationship, but after my night away with Marco I began to wonder if that's what I really wanted.

There were two occasions during the calendar year when New York City private schools made a bigger push than usual for donations: the first Tuesday after Thanksgiving, (aka #GivingTuesday) and the annual spring benefit/auction in the middle of May.

Although my son's school served children with diverse needs, its fundraising efforts rivaled those of any mainstream private institution. I had no idea what to expect from a benefit/auction, but I was told it was a night for parents to get all dressed up, have some drinks and finger foods, and bid for donated items like vacations and jewelry.

This was Henry's second year at the school, but last year's event had been virtual, so at first, I thought it might be fun to go in person. Then I remembered curriculum night, movie night, and family game night and concluded it might not be such a good idea after all. As one of the few single parents at those events, those nights only highlighted how different I was from everyone else. I'd felt very alone, and I didn't know many of the other parents or teachers anyway. Still, the auction might be fun if Marco would come with me.

We hadn't seen each other in three weeks, since the night at the hotel, but we still exchanged texts several times a week. I decided to take a risk and ask him if he wanted to join me. I was sure he was going to say no, either because he was otherwise occupied, or he just didn't want to go. But I was delighted when he said yes. I felt so relieved I didn't have to show up alone to an event where everyone else would be with their spouse.

I honestly could not remember the last time I'd gotten dressed up for a night out and I was excited. I was also nervous because Marco and I hadn't spent much time out in public together. Of course we spent a good amount of time talking, we just happened to be naked most of that time.

I already felt like an outsider with the other parents. When Steven was alive, he did drop-off and pickup. He was the involved parent, the one who volunteered for things and made playdates. He was the one who made friends with the other parents, not me. At that time, I had been working my ass off to make sure we had health insurance.

Even though most of Henry's classmates had been in school together since the first grade, he blended right in when he started in third grade. He was always a leader in school because he was smart, and other kids were interested in learning from him. His challenges were social-emotional, but he was thriving in his school's therapeutic environment with small class sizes.

Since I wasn't really friends with anyone, I didn't care too much about what the other parents or teachers might think of me bringing a date. For all I knew, maybe they were all unhappy in their decade-old marriages. They might even be jealous to see me with a hot younger man.

This occasion called for a new dress, so I went shopping down the block at Bloomingdale's Outlet. I liked the store, but it could be hit or miss. Sometimes I found items I loved but couldn't find my size; other times there just wasn't anything I liked.

I got lucky relatively early in my search with an off-the-shoulder black taffeta dress. It had ruffles all around the bodice and fit very slim through the waist, hips, and legs, ending just below the knee.

The evening of the benefit I told Marco to meet me outside the upscale restaurant the school had reserved for the event. It was very close to my apartment, but I wasn't ready for him to meet my son, or for my son to meet him.

I almost felt like I was making a triumphant return to the school's social scene, and I wanted to look my best. I booked a couple of appointments for hair and makeup through the Glam squad app, and they did not disappoint.

Henry was not impressed when he and Jane got home from his after-school sports program, but she said I looked "amazing." I had to admit, not being picked up at my apartment felt a little anticlimactic, but I didn't want to open the "dating" can of worms, not yet anyway.

The weather had finally turned warm toward the end of May, so I didn't mind waiting outside for a couple of minutes until Marco arrived. I knew he was taking the subway, so I was looking for him in the direction of the nearest station.

When I heard someone call my name, I turned around and saw him walking toward me. Was he walking slowly or had my brain been set to slow motion? The light wind blew his jet-black hair away from his face, and I noticed he was wearing a black T-shirt under a black sports jacket with black jeans. On any other man it might have been a little too Johnny Cash, but he looked gorgeous.

Marco was a man who was used to being noticed, especially by the middle-aged moms on the days he picked up his daughter from school. That's what he'd told me and seeing him now I could believe it. I couldn't take my eyes off all six feet two inches of him.

"Wow," I said. "You look very handsome."

"Thank you," he answered. "You look pretty."

I wasn't sure how to greet him out here in the real world, so we did the half hug and kiss on the cheek thing. It was a little awkward, but we both laughed and then went inside. We headed straight for the bar and got two glasses of red wine before mingling with the crowd.

"I don't know that many people here," I said just before the mother of one of Henry's friends came over to say hello.

"Hi Amy, it's so good to see you here."

"Thanks Liz," I said before introducing her to Marco.

She gave me a wide-eyed look, followed by a double eyebrow lift that I interpreted to mean, "He's hot, good for you," before we moved on.

I was glad we grabbed a few hors d'oeuvres before the auction started since we hadn't had dinner. I didn't know what to expect (bidding wars?), but it turned out to be boring.

Matt would have been perfect in a situation like this—he was a naughty risk taker like me. Instead of listening to the head of school auction off designer handbags, we would have been fucking in the bathroom, probably for the second or third time.

It was such a shame that his wife didn't appreciate that side of him, but I guess living with a horny man-child all the time could become tedious. There had to be some sort of in between, right?

We ended up leaving a little early since Marco had a long ride home. I thought we both had a good time, but I left feeling more confused about our "relationship." I didn't initiate any PDA because I wasn't sure he would welcome it, although I very much wished he had put his arm around me or held my hand. I felt so tentative with him in public, scared of overstepping an unspoken boundary.

Marco and I were not a real couple, but I felt myself wanting more of an attachment. I kept thinking that the more time we spent together, the closer we would become, but I was so unsure of myself, of where I stood with him. I was scared to tell him that I wanted more for fear he wouldn't want to see me at all. There was a desperation that lived in my body at the thought of never seeing him again.

At the same time, I felt the need for control over the situation. It felt awful that he could just disappear anytime, even though he never said he would do that. I hated that we had no concrete plans to see each other again, and it was torture living with the ambiguity. My nervous system was warning me to run away from him while I still felt strong enough to lose him.

A line from Taylor Swift's *I Did Something Bad* went through my head on repeat: "You gotta leave before you get left."

When June began, I hadn't seen Marco in a couple of weeks (since the auction), and I started to miss him in a way that made me feel very vulnerable. There was a connection between losing Steven and the fear I had of losing Marco, but I didn't fully understand it.

I was vaguely familiar with the psychological term "transference," when someone redirects their feelings about one person onto someone else, although I didn't necessarily have a sense of awareness about this at that time. In retrospect I can see it clearly, but back then I was just trying to navigate my complicated emotions the best I could while managing the rest of my life at the same time.

With the end of the school year only two weeks away, I began to feel anxious about upcoming grief milestones, especially the one-year anniversary of Steven's death on the 25th of August. But even before that, in July, I had to get through my first birthday without my husband, as well as what would have been our fourteenth wedding anniversary.

When Steven died, I hadn't let myself feel anything; I just went into action mode. I had shit to get done, and I did it. Now, it was becoming clearer to me that I wanted a real connection with a man who said he didn't want a relationship, which made me wonder if I was just setting myself up for more heartbreak. I didn't want to give up the sense of safety and comfort I had when Marco and I were together, but I also didn't want to constantly question how he felt about me when we were apart. I wondered at times if he was seeing other women, but I thought I would sense it if he was.

It wasn't fair to give Marco an ultimatum, but the ambiguous nature of our relationship was becoming unbearable for me. I wished I could have forced him to choose all or nothing, hoping he chose the former rather than the latter. The truth was that I had little control over my own feelings, let alone his.

CHAPTER TWENTY-ONE

TIME ALWAYS sped up toward the end of the school year, and by the second week in June, parents shook their heads in disbelief that time had gone by so fast. I was no different, but the added weight of my relationship (or lack thereof) with Marco was making my head spin.

I talked about these feelings with my therapist, and she suggested I try the Mood notes app. It used cognitive behavioral therapy techniques to challenge negative thoughts and feelings by looking at different thinking traps. I used it when I felt particularly anxious about Marco.

Which negative emotions are you feeling?

Angry / Ashamed / Disappointed / Lonely / Sad / Tired

What's happening at the moment?

I told Marco that I didn't want to be with other men, and he said he wouldn't stop "anyone" from feeling their feelings. He said he was clear that he wasn't ready for a relationship, but he hoped it didn't have to be all or nothing between us.

I told him it had to be nothing, but the next day I was so miserable without him. I didn't want to settle for less, but no one else cared about me, except for Matt, who was married. I was scared to be alone in a way I never had been before. I wanted so badly to be strong, like I was in every other aspect of my life, but I felt like another piece of myself was being ripped away.

I left him a voice message that morning, crying. When Steven died, I had lost my sense of stability and no matter how much I was trying, I couldn't get it back. The panic I felt at the thought of losing Marco was greater than preserving any false sense of pride I had. I was grateful he replied even though he said I wasn't being nice and had caused a lot of unnecessary drama. He said we should have a period of no contact and then maybe have coffee and talk. He needed me to give him time, and he would contact me when he was ready.

What thought went through your mind that contributed most to your negative feeling?

I was ashamed about how much I missed him when we weren't together because I knew he didn't feel the same way. I felt worthless. Every man since Steven died had left me, but Marco was the only man (besides married Matt) who wanted to see me more than once. I told myself that meant something, and I was so desperate to feel like I belonged with someone again.

Blaming / Fortune Telling / Emotional Reasoning

What's another way of thinking about the situation without traps?

Instead, I could have given myself grace, acknowledging that I had so much loss over the last four years. It was understandable that I wanted Marco to step into the huge void left when Steven died.

Now that you have modified your thinking, has the intensity of your feelings changed?

Not much had changed, but I was 10 percent less angry. I supposed that was something.

As more time passed since Steven died, instead of feeling more grounded and like my old self, the less I recognized who I used to be. I was slowly breaking down, stripped of my role as wife, still unable to function at work, and stuck waiting for a man to tell me whether he'd have me in his life again or not.

Who was I?

I took my final leave from work through September. If I didn't return after that I would lose my job. How was it possible to love my work so much one day, and not care about it at all seemingly overnight?

Maybe after the one-year anniversary of Steven's death at the end of August I would want to go back. Once upon a time I believed that grief ended at the year mark, and who's to say it doesn't? But until then I couldn't decide either way about my employment situation.

Summer used to be my favorite season, but now it felt like floating on a wooden raft in the middle of the ocean. I was small and insignificant, and so angry to be at the mercy of the wind and currents, counting on them to safely deliver me back to a shore that was no longer visible.

When my life felt out of control, putting together a photo-shoot was the one thing that could get me out of my head and focused on my body. Once I set up my phone, ring light, and tripod, I began my transformation by working my way down from head to toe. I still had my decades-old Vidal Sassoon ceramic curling iron, which gave my hair some body while smoothing out the frizz. Then I'd do my makeup before putting on my lingerie or sexy costume. I'd recently purchased a sparkly red, blue, and gold Wonder Woman bustier that I paired with a red g-string and five-inch silver platform shoes. I could barely stand in them, let alone walk, so I had to make sure there was always something nearby I could lean on. When I saw the photos, I decided the shoes were worth risking a broken bone because they made my legs and my ass look amazing.

Marco was going to Italy for several weeks with his daughter at the end of June. I hadn't expected to hear from him while he was away even before we stopped speaking. I honestly didn't know our status beyond waiting to be contacted whenever he decided he had enough time to forgive me. I felt miserable, but I had no other choice if I wanted to see him again.

I longed for some stability, and I broke down and texted him. I felt desperate to know if he ever wanted to see me again, and I didn't care if that made me seem pathetic.

Amy: Hi Marco, I guess you changed your mind about coffee with me. I didn't mean to upset you. I'm sorry you felt I was unkind. I was really hurting.

Marco: I haven't changed my mind about meeting with you, Amy. I just haven't found the right time. You told me you'd wait until I was ready to talk.

All I cared about was that he hadn't changed his mind. I felt relieved that he'd replied, even if he was annoyed that I hadn't given him more time. I tried to explain how hard it had been living with the unknown of Steven's terminal cancer diagnosis. For three years we lived from scan to scan, not knowing when the news would be catastrophic.

Maybe I was never an especially patient person, but it was hell not knowing when I would have the rug pulled out from beneath my feet. With Steven's cancer we pretended it wasn't really happening and carried on as normal, but that wasn't an option for me anymore. I was not okay waiting for everything to fall apart. I had to know *now* what would happen so I could protect myself.

I felt too vulnerable to ask him outright, "When am I going to see you again?" after he told me not to contact him. I hoped he might decide to see me sooner rather than later if I reminded him that our consecutive vacations (mine began the following week) meant we wouldn't see each other for a month.

Amy: Okay Marco. I'll give you more space. I'm sorry. I probably won't see you until you return from Italy in July. I hope you have a wonderful trip with your daughter.

Marco: I'm not leaving until the end of the month. Are you free to meet this Friday?

It worked. Not only would he see me, but I only had to wait a few days. A sense of relief washed over me, and I said yes, even though I was ashamed of my neediness.

Amy: It's supposed to be a beautiful day. Do you want to go for a walk in Riverside Park?

Marco: Alright. That's a nice idea.

Friday's weather was glorious. Bluebird skies for miles punctuated by the noontime sun directly overhead. The breeze off the Hudson River ruffled our hair as we walked along the path that spanned the length of the West Side of Manhattan.

"You were right," Marco said. "It is a beautiful day."

We continued along the path uptown from 72nd to 86th Street in companionable silence. There were a lot more people out on the running and bike paths than I expected on a Friday afternoon.

It was the first real summer-like day of the season, and everyone wanted to be outside enjoying it. We stopped at a water fountain and then decided to sit on one of the benches facing the river.

Trees had been planted at regular intervals, creating canopies of leafy shade. It was a much-needed respite from the heat rising off the concrete beneath our feet. We sat next to each other, looking out at the river for a few minutes before I turned to him and said, "I'm glad you're here."

I was more than glad, I was grateful. Letting go of my pride was a price I was willing to pay to avoid the chaos and panic I felt without him.

"I'm glad I'm here too," he said.

We talked about our summer plans: his trip to Italy, my Airbnb rental in a nearby suburb for the two weeks between Henry's last day of school and his first day of camp. Jane would be coming with us, and we'd have some of Henry's friends visit for a day to swim.

After about an hour and a half, Marco walked me home and we kissed passionately before saying goodbye. While I was so happy we had repaired our relationship, I was upset that we hadn't made plans to see each other again in July.

CHAPTER TWENTY-TWO

WHEN WE left for our vacation, I was grateful to have Jane with us, but it wasn't the same as traveling with my husband for several reasons. On a practical level, we no longer had our car or our driver. Jane didn't have an American driver's license, and I didn't drive. We were able to get to and from the Airbnb by Uber, but once there we stayed at the house.

Then there were the obvious differences between traveling as a family of three versus an employer, their child, and an employee. Jane was like family, and we were good friends, but the reality was that I was paying her to accompany us. We also slept in our own bedrooms, and she wasn't on call twenty-four seven the way parents are with their children.

The trip itself started off fine. The house was a bit outdated, but what we really came for was the pool. I hadn't been sure about going away for the first time without Steven, so I'd ended up booking the house last minute. I knew from experience that it could take the homeowner's pool company a few days to get it ready for use at the beginning of the summer.

When we arrived, the pool hadn't been officially "opened" yet, and it was uncovered and full of leaves, debris, and cloudy water. The homeowner, who was abroad for a wedding, assured us that it would be available for use within a few days. Two days later, a couple of guys from the pool maintenance company arrived, but they said it would take another week to balance the chemicals so we could go swimming.

I thanked them for letting me know and then had a breakdown back in the house. All I could think was that if Steven were with us this wouldn't be happening. I knew that wasn't a rational thought, but that's how I felt. I unraveled as I realized we would only have three days of pool use out of the two weeks I had rented the house, and that was a best-case scenario.

How could this be happening? I didn't want Jane to see me fall apart completely so I went into the bathroom to cry. I hated that stupid house, its owner, the pool, and myself for renting such a horrible place. Thank goodness I had reconciled with Marco, and he was still in the United States.

Amy: Everything is horrible. The house is old, and we can't use the pool for another week! This wouldn't be happening if Steven were here! I fucking hate this!

Marco: That sounds so frustrating, I'm so sorry.

Amy: I'm about to kill the owner of this house, but if anyone finds this text I'm speaking metaphorically.

We ended up staying at the house for a few more days, but when the pool guys didn't come back to finish with the chemicals, we packed up and went home early. Our first vacation without Steven sucked, and I felt defeated, sad, and lonely.

Henry started his school's six-week summer program at the end of June. It was more day camp and less academics, and we were both relieved to resume our familiar routine. I wouldn't hear from Marco for the next two weeks while he was traveling, so I went on Feeld to find someone to chat with.

I scrolled through the guys who liked me and thought I saw a familiar face. It was another redhead, but it turned out not to be Joel or Ed. His name was John, but he really did look like the other two guys. When I saw he was also thirty-eight years old I thought I might be going crazy.

We chatted on the app for a while before moving over to texting on our phones once I verified his identity. John was a nice guy, a nurse who was recently divorced and exploring his options. He lived in upper Manhattan, which made it convenient for us to meet on his next day off, the day after tomorrow.

The heat wasn't supposed to become oppressive until the late afternoon, so I suggested we meet in Riverside Park. I thought, *Why not try something different?* I wasn't sure what I was looking for anyway.

I missed Marco, but I still didn't know where I stood with him. He was also away on another continent, and I didn't know when I would see him again.

John seemed nice enough, but I hadn't had much luck with redheads.

What I really wanted was Steven. I missed him terribly, but he was gone, and he wasn't coming back.

On the morning I met John in the park, it was already ninety degrees by 10 a.m. So much for not becoming oppressive until the afternoon. There was no respite from the heat, so we grabbed a couple of iced coffees and went back to my climate-controlled apartment.

John was easy to talk to, and we fell into an easy discussion about what it was like to be single in New York City. He was exploring his sexual desires just like I was, and he was so recently divorced that I had no illusions that he was looking for anything more than sex.

I hadn't been sure about my intentions for meeting John in the first place. Yes, I was lonely without Marco. At the same time, I felt like he was giving me mixed signals. He said he didn't want a relationship, but before he left for Italy, we had been texting almost every day. We talked about everything: his work, my ambivalence about mine, our kids, and a lot about sex. We had great sex, but when we started meeting each other outside of the bedroom I thought maybe we could have something more. But just when I started thinking we were getting closer, he went away and didn't say anything about staying in contact. We had no plans to see each other again, and I felt scared that he could just walk away and leave me alone. I tried to end it with him first because it was too painful and frightening not knowing when or if he would disappear. We were in a strange kind of limbo that was difficult for me to tolerate. And of course, I hadn't heard from him since he left for his trip.

I felt more vulnerable than ever, which led me to looking for, and finding, someone else. It was an impulsive decision based on the fear of being left alone again, and now John was here, and he was kind and cute. What would it hurt to spend an hour feeling close to another adult?

There was definite chemistry between us, and when he leaned over to kiss me, I reciprocated. I wasn't in the mood to pretend we were lovers and have languid, sensual sex, but I didn't want to get my ass beaten either. John was happy to follow my lead as I took my clothes off, jumped into his arms, and wrapped my legs tightly around his waist. It was fine, but with zero emotional connection. I didn't think I'd see him again.

Later that day, after I picked up Henry from camp, I got the most wonderful surprise! My phone vibrated and I saw I had a text from . . . Marco! He had only been gone a couple days and now he was texting me from Italy! I closed my eyes and saw his smile and I smiled back. The relief was intense, and I felt myself tearing up. He wasn't gone forever. I was so happy he wanted to maintain the connection with me while he was so far away. He wanted to keep me in his life as much as I wanted him in mine.

Marco: We just finished a sixty-mile bike tour in ninety-degree heat. Here we are.

He attached a photo of them in their bicycle gear, smiling.

Amy: Omg! I'm so proud of you both!

Marco: Thanks. How are you doing?

Amy: I'm great! It's so good to hear from you.

For the rest of his trip, he continued to text me photos and bits of news about their adventures. I couldn't have been happier, and I knew just how I wanted to welcome him home.

Amy: Babe, let's celebrate our birthdays when you get back.

Marco: That sounds like a good idea.

Amy: Lmk when you have a night off from work and daddy duty. I already have something in mind.

It never occurred to me that I should feel guilty about sleeping with John, and I didn't see any reason to tell Marco. We never talked about being exclusive, and besides, I had no idea that he wanted to stay connected while he was away. As far as I knew he wasn't even thinking about me, and I reasoned that had I known he was, I wouldn't have slept with John.

It had to mean *something* that Marco wanted to stay in touch with me while on vacation five thousand miles away. I would only have done that with someone I really cared about, someone who was important to me.

We weren't boyfriend and girlfriend, but that didn't seem out of the realm of possibility one day. We had agreed to be honest about who we were connecting with sexually, but he never so much as mentioned another woman. Wouldn't I know if he was dating someone else? I continued to assume that he would have mentioned it if he was sleeping with someone else.

I wasn't fooling myself into believing Marco loved me, but that didn't mean he never would. One of my favorite songs from the 1980s, "Never Say Never," was by the band Romeo Void and it summed up my feelings perfectly. I couldn't wait until he got home.

CHAPTER TWENTY-THREE

THREE WEEKS later, in mid-July, I eagerly awaited Marco's arrival in our room at the Mandarin Hotel. I knew he would enjoy the spectacular view of Central Park from the fiftieth floor as much as I did, and I couldn't wait to see him again.

I took a photo and sent it to Lisa.

Amy: Waiting for Marco, but in the meantime not a bad view.

Lisa: Love it! Enjoy yourself ;)

I didn't want Marco to waste time looking for street parking, so I reserved a spot for him in the garage next door. I knew he was a grown man, fully capable of parking his own car, but in my experience, most men would rather spend thirty minutes circling the streets of New York praying to the parking gods than spend $30 for an easy spot in a garage. He couldn't stay the whole night (he had to be at work by 6 a.m.), but I could still enjoy the morning alone and treat myself to my favorite breakfast of bagels and lox the next day. In the meantime, I wanted him for as long as I could have him.

Amy: I know you can't stay, but it costs the same to park overnight as it does for a couple of hours.

Marco: Thanks babe. I'm on my way. I should be there in forty-five minutes.

If I was being completely honest, I would have paid double that amount for an extra half hour with Marco. Suddenly, I felt my face flush with the hot sting of shame. I made it sound like I was paying him to spend time with me.

No, I told myself, as I shook the thought away. He was coming because I'd planned a little birthday celebration for the two of us. His birthday was last week, and mine was coming up in a few days.

It would also have been my fourteenth wedding anniversary, but I didn't want to focus on what I lost. That would have been excruciating and ruined my precious time with Marco. So, I did my best not to even think about Steven or my wedding.

The first thing I liked to do when I got up to a hotel room was to strip naked and put on one of the plush bathrobes hanging in the closet. It was a signal to my nervous system that I was safe and could relax. There wasn't anything else I should be doing and nowhere else I had to be.

Although Matt and I hadn't seen each other in several months, our connection was strong and we still sexted often. When I told him I was going to celebrate my birthday with Marco at the Mandarin Hotel, he said we should rent some porn. *Okay, why not*? I thought. I still had about thirty minutes until Marco arrived, so I grabbed the TV remote and made myself comfortable on the bed.

I clicked through to the in-room movie section and scrolled to the adult category. There wasn't a lot to choose from, but what they did have was a step up from Porn Hub. I read each movie's synopsis and choose a French movie with English subtitles.

The closed captioning font was too small for me to see clearly from the head of the bed where I was propped up on four fluffy down pillows. I doubted it mattered if I understood what the actors were saying. I was about to press play when I realized I'd left Lulu and my lube in the suitcase. Ugh.

I shimmied awkwardly on my butt to the side of the king size bed. I wasn't used to navigating such a large mattress; Steven and I had been comfortable with our queen-size sleigh bed. I got what I needed from the suitcase and crawled back to my spot, resting up against the mountain of feather pillows.

I had no idea what was going on in the movie, but for the first fifteen minutes there wasn't anything to indicate it was pornographic. All I knew was that the main character was a beautiful woman in her late thirties or early forties. She looked gorgeous, wearing tall white boots and a short backless halter-style dress. She put on a mask and straightened her dress as a man held the tall door open for her. She walked inside and saw groups of naked men and women fucking.

Finally, time to power up Lulu, I thought to myself.

As I took off my robe, the door to the room swung open and Marco strode in. He paused at the foot of the bed, swiveling his head back and forth between me and the TV. He stopped to look at me and I saw that smile, the one that lit up his whole face. And now, I felt lit up too.

"Perfect timing babe," I said, holding out Lulu to him. "I was just getting started."

"What are we watching?" he asked, pulling his T-shirt up and over his head.

"French porn," I said, followed by a brief synopsis of the plot thus far.

I watched as Marco kicked off his shoes, stepped out of his jeans and boxers, and crawled toward me naked from the foot of the bed. I thought he was leaning in to kiss me, but he said, "Babe, I can stay the night. I just have to leave by 5:30 a.m."

"That's amazing!"

I kept my eyes on the screen, watching the orgy that had just gotten underway, but inside I was jumping up and down with joy.

"Oh!" Marco had followed my gaze but wasn't expecting to see a close-up of our protagonist being double penetrated by two well-endowed younger men.

"Are they wearing condoms?" I asked. "Is that an EU porn thing?"

"I don't know," Marco said, turning over and propping himself up on the pillows beside me. "At least they're being safe."

"Do you wear condoms with the other women you're fucking?" I asked, eyes still on the TV.

I couldn't look at him, I felt incredibly vulnerable. I remembered our conversation about protection, but at that moment my insecurity made me wonder if he'd slept with other women but hadn't told me. Fuck. I wished I had kept my mouth shut.

"I thought that's what we agreed on," he said matter-of-factly.

After five months together I'd begun to think of us as primary partners. He certainly was the most important man in my life. But I questioned if I was the most important woman in his life, and it was on the tip of my tongue to ask him *who* he had been fucking.

Before I could pose the question, the doorbell chimed, and a man's voice boomed, "Room service!" I was grateful for the interruption. I didn't want to appear jealous and possessive, and besides, when would he even have time to fuck anyone else? Between his work, nights with his daughter, and me, his schedule was full.

I yelled back, "Just a minute! We'll be right there!"

I scrambled to put on my robe and whispered, "There's another one in the closet."

Marco jumped up, threw open the closet door, and pulled the robe off the hanger.

"You ordered something for us?" he asked, jamming his long arms into the sleeves.

"Yes," I said as I opened the door.

The man in the doorway seemed short compared to Marco, but he was probably average height. He was holding a plate with an elegant mini tart topped with fresh strawberries in one hand and a small bottle of champagne in the other.

"May I put these down for you?" he said, gesturing toward the small coffee table by the window.

"Yes, please," I said, taking a step back to let him in.

As I turned around, I almost bumped into Marco who was standing right behind me. Why did he have that sheepish grin on his face? I looked past him and saw that the movie had been paused, rather than turned off, the climactic moment frozen on the screen.

I shrugged my shoulders as I reached for my bag, pulling a $10 bill from my wallet. "Thank you," I said, handing it to the room service attendant.

"Thank you," he said, smiling.

I thought he was about to leave, but he continued, "It's very good to spend time alone as a couple . . . *without* the children. I know, I've been married for twenty-five years."

Marco and I smiled and nodded.

He continued, "Whose birthday are we celebrating?"

I didn't know what to say, but I liked the idea that this complete stranger thought we were a couple.

"Well, actually . . ." Marco began.

I thought he was going to tell the attendant we weren't really "together," but instead he said, "We're celebrating both of our birthdays. They're only a few days apart."

"Oh, that's wonderful!" he said, beaming. "Your energy is a good match for each other, which is also important for a long and happy marriage."

There was an awkward silence before Marco asked, "You know a lot about sustaining a long-term relationship. What else should we know?"

The two men chatted, but I wasn't listening anymore. Just for a moment, a few seconds at most, I let myself imagine what it would feel like to be loved by Marco. I imagined feeling lighter, freed from carrying the weight of my constant doubts and insecurities. I felt the ease with which I could move through the world again, knowing there was someone who always had my back.

I also felt a pang of fear. Would I feel tied down, or was I just scared of another loss? I could feel the muscles in my jaw tightening as I thought about being left again. For all the betrayal I felt when Steven was diagnosed with cancer, I knew he didn't want to leave me.

Charged by the push-pull of both positive and negative polarities, I was poised to run either toward a new life or away from the possibility of pain. How could I feel safe with someone while also maintaining my autonomy?

"Amy? Do we need anything else?" Marco asked, interrupting my thoughts.

"Nope, we're good," I said, bouncing slowly on the balls of my feet.

I locked the door after the attendant left and turned to Marco.

"That was interesting," I said, "but I really need you to feed me some tart now."

"Right now?" he said, undoing the tie on his robe.

The front swung open, and I saw that he was hard.

"I guess I can wait a little while longer," I said, opening my robe, and letting it slide off my shoulders and onto the floor.

I picked up the remote, which Marco had left in front of the TV after he paused it, and crawled back up to my pile of pillows resting against the headboard.

"Should we try a few of these moves?" I asked, pointing the remote at the TV and pressing "play."

"I think we should," he said, joining me, "and then we can have our birthday treat."

His kisses were long and slow, but I had already waited so long. I kissed him back harder, more insistently, using my body to push him onto his back. He looked at me as if to say, *Oh really. That's how it's going to be?*

I put my hands on his chest, bracing myself as I straddled him.

As I lowered myself down, using one of my hands to guide his hardness inside me, I thought, *Yes, this is how it's going to be. I love strawberry tarts and champagne, but this year, you are my birthday treat.*

CHAPTER TWENTY-FOUR

I KNEW OUR August Airbnb rental would be a huge success. This time around, Henry and I went to visit the place *before* I signed the rental agreement. The hosts were lovely, the pool filter worked, and the water was heated.

Amy: Good morning! I'm going to spend a couple of days by the pool at our new Airbnb. Do you want to hang out with me? Bring your bathing suit.

Marco: I have Sam for a couple of days, she has another orthodontist appointment.

Amy: Bring her with you. It will just be the three of us. Henry will be in the city with Jane finishing up his last week of day camp.

Marco: Okay, I think she would like that.

I was glad that Marco and his daughter Sam could visit on a day when I would be at the house alone. I wanted to get to know her a little better before I included Henry. I was always anxious about introducing him to people who were outside of our special needs community. Not everyone was familiar with the concept of neurodivergence, so I did my best to protect him from situations where people might be judgmental or even inadvertently hurtful.

Chronologically, Sam was only a few months older than my son, but they were born in different calendar years, so she was a grade ahead. Girls also matured faster than boys. I sometimes wondered if boys ever caught up.

I got in an Uber after I dropped Henry off at school and headed to the house. It was only a thirty-minute drive from Manhattan, but it felt like eons away from the noise, crowds, and blistering concrete sidewalks in New York City. It felt huge after living in two- or three-bedroom apartments my entire life. The living room's double-height ceilings added to the vastness of the space, yet it also felt cozy. A large leather couch had been draped with soft blankets and throw pillows and faced the largest flat-screen TV I had ever seen.

Marco and Sam were due to arrive at 11 a.m., but I wanted to get there a couple of hours early so I'd have enough time to cool down the house and warm up the pool. After I lowered the thermostat inside, I went outside and flipped on the pool heater. I got a pretty good workout skimming the leaves and bugs off the surface of the water. The pool guys came once a week to vacuum anything that sank to the bottom and balance the pH levels, but since it had been five days since their last visit, a good amount of debris had accumulated.

Back in the house, it felt a little scary to be there alone. I began to understand how overwhelming it was for my widowed friends who owned single family homes and property. From the roof to the sewer lines, there was a lot to take care of, not including the backyard landscaping. It made sense that a lot of people downsized after their kids got married and had children of their own.

Just then, I heard a car pull up in the driveway and then a couple of doors slammed. I recognized Sam from the photos

Marco had shared with me, so I wasn't surprised by how little she was. At her age, on the cusp of puberty, girls who had gotten their first period often looked more like older teens or twentysomethings, but Sam still had a girl's body, just like I did at that age.

"Hello and welcome," I said as they got out of the car.

"Hello Amy. This is Sam," he said as she took a half step behind him.

I had no idea what he'd told her about me, but I assumed very little. I was probably one of his "friends," which I'm sure Sam knew was code for "daddy's fuckbot" or whatever the tween girls were calling it these days. Or maybe she was more innocent, like Henry.

"Come on inside," I said. "Let me give you a tour."

After offering them glasses of water I showed them around the first floor. Adjacent to the kitchen was the dining area, dominated by a large rectangular table made of dark metal. Just beyond that black behemoth was a small bedroom and the floor's only bathroom.

I led them downstairs to the finished basement with its large couch with built-in cup holders, reclining seats, and footrests. It too was in front of a large TV, but this one was hooked up to an Xbox and a PlayStation.

Along one wall there were built-in shelves filled with books and board games, all of which looked like they hadn't been touched in a while. Behind the couch was an actual air-hockey table, like the kind found in an arcade.

"Do you guys want to play?" I asked, holding up the plug which would turn on the air part of the game. Sam's face lit up in what I expected was the same joy and wonder I had when discovering that people had arcade games in their homes.

"Yes!" she said. "Do you want to play?"

She was asking me to play with her. Yay!

I soon learned that Sam was competitive, just like her father. She put her weight into thwacking the puck in my direction, defeating me easily.

"C'mon Dad, let's play."

Marco gave me a look that said, *Is it okay?* and I nodded back.

I handed him my paddle and the two went at it. *Thwack! Thwack, thwack!*

All I could think was that my overly competitive son would have fit right in. Me, not so much.

There was some good-natured ribbing between them, but Marco wasn't going to let his daughter win. After he won a second game, I suggested we go back upstairs where they could change into their bathing suits before going out to the pool.

Sam wanted her privacy, so I sent her upstairs to the kid's bathroom. Matt would have had me bent over the couch the second she was out of sight, but Marco went into the downstairs bedroom to change. I would have preferred if he had taken my hand and led me to the bedroom with him—not for full-on sex, but for a few moments of intimacy before spending the day with his daughter.

We headed out through the French doors to the backyard. It wasn't massive but somehow managed to accommodate a midsize inground pool, a picnic table with a large sun umbrella sprouting from a hole in its center, a stand-alone hammock, and a children's swing set, without feeling overcrowded.

We set up our towels on the lounge chairs before going in to play monkey in the middle and shoot baskets into a non-regulation-sized net. I could tell Sam liked me by the way she enthusiastically answered all my questions about her school and her friends. I was grateful not to be completely oblivious to the tween scene.

I got out of the pool to order sushi for a late lunch, pleasantly surprised that Sam liked it. Henry never ate cooked fish, let alone raw. I knew I shouldn't compare, but it made me wish my son and I had more interests in common, even if we just liked some of the same foods.

I was a little jealous of my friends who had daughters they could bond with over music, movies, and makeup. I felt like my time was running out to bond with Henry as an adolescent. Time was moving so fast and before I knew it, he would only want to hang out with his friends.

I caught myself watching them and I felt a bit wistful, remembering the difficult relationship I had with my own father, and how that drove me to find a man who would be a better one to our own child. I found him, and then I lost him.

I wanted that back for Henry so badly, and I wanted it for me too. What would I do when he ditched me for his friends? That's what my brother and I did to my mom and stepfather. It was a normal part of growing up and becoming independent.

I began to wonder about the possibility of rebuilding my family with Marco. We were slowly getting closer, and he had introduced me to his daughter. I could tell that Sam liked me, and I liked her too. It didn't seem out of the realm of possibility if he was good with Henry.

It was almost 4 p.m. by the time we finished eating, and Marco and Sam needed to head back into the city. I decided to stay at the house overnight to get some more pool time the following morning.

We all changed back into our clothes, and I double checked that they had everything before I walked them out to their car.

"We'll be here all of August if you'd like to come back," I said. "You both have an open invitation."

"Yes! Dad, let's come back!" Sam said excitedly.

"We'll have to figure out a time that works for all of us," Marco told her.

"Just let me know . . ." I let my voice trail off.

They got in the car. I waved as they drove off.

I felt lonely.

I was keenly aware of how much I wanted them to stay.

Or wished they had taken me with them.

CHAPTER TWENTY-FIVE

BY LATE August, my relationship with Matt had slowly morphed into a close friendship. I even shared with him my ideas about doing something with my photography.

Amy: I'm thinking about becoming a midlife influencer on Instagram. I don't plan to fade away into decrepitude until I die. I want to show women that they still have so much life left to live.

Matt: That's a great idea; you will be so good at that. I think you could make a lot of money on OnlyFans, but I support whatever you do.

Matt believed that I could be very successful on OnlyFans, but I wanted to use Instagram to build an online gallery of the photos and non-NSFW videos I was creating. I felt I had an important message to share with midlife women about this part of our lives when we were all reinventing ourselves after decades of focusing on children and family.

I knew Matt cared about me, and I believed on some level we even loved each other, but there was no romantic partnership in our future. He was traveling with his wife and kids that summer which gave us a break from our virtual connection (I hadn't seen him in person in months), as well as time for me to reevaluate what I wanted from a relationship.

It was always my hope that Matt would truly appreciate everything he had and stop cheating on his wife, but I wasn't sure he could. He had compartmentalized his life completely, to the extent that he didn't think that what he was doing was dishonest.

I wished we didn't have to keep our friendship a secret, and that I could be a part of his life without sneaking around. Of course, that was impossible because of how we met and the intimacy we had shared. The lies I told myself to keep him in my life, that I wasn't to blame for his infidelity, were beginning to feel worse than the lies he told his wife. As I built my influencer platform on Instagram and enjoyed my time in the pool with Henry, I came to the realization that Matt and I were done as lovers.

By the end of August my year of "firsts" without Steven officially came to an end. I'd leapt over every hurdle, from Henry's first day of fourth grade to what should have been our fourteenth wedding anniversary. I had deftly cleared them all. I felt like I had run a marathon, and now it was time to receive my medal.

One year ago, as I held his hand and played Shawn Colvin's *Sunny Came Home,* Steven took his last breath. I walked into that hospital as a wife, and I came out as a widow. I hadn't been expecting that to happen, not that day.

While I was in shock I felt other emotions as well. To be honest, I had been terrified of bringing Steven home to die. Where would I put a hospital bed? How would I manage his pain if he had any? I would have had to hire home health aides to help me, but that meant strangers in and out of the apartment. My home would no longer have felt like a sanctuary.

So, there was a part of me that felt grateful that he'd died in the hospital, quietly and without pain. More than that, I was relieved that the terrible thing had happened, and after three years of treatment and scans, it was over.

Does that mean I was happy Steven died? Of course not, but the event, his death, and the feeling, my relief, were in some ways inextricably intertwined. Death did us part, and I still felt gratitude that I didn't have to watch him fade away in our home.

Henry, Jane, and I loved our summer rental, especially the pool. This Airbnb was everything the last one was not, and I felt like I had redeemed myself as the family vacation organizer, even if our family looked very different than it did a year ago.

Today I was a stranger in a stranger's home. I was surrounded by people that Henry and I didn't know a year ago . . . people that Steven would never know, and yet they had become constants in our lives.

One bright afternoon Jane was taking photographs from her lounge chair while Marco, Sam, Henry, and I played in the pool. This was the day they were able to come back for a visit, so I told myself that Steven would be happy to see the light again in his son's eyes, and in mine.

I looked around and realized I had created this scene from nothing. I'd scouted the location and auditioned players for each part. I'd written the script and directed the actors, but now I began to think that the play I'd produced could become a reality. Was it so farfetched that we could become a family?

"Girls against the boys!" Sam yelled as we set up for another round of monkeys in the middle.

"Okay, we need a strategy," I whispered in Sam's ear. "Your dad has an unfair height advantage, so don't throw the ball directly to me. I can swim for it faster than he can."

Sam nodded her head and smiled as I took my place at the deep end of the pool. My strategy worked for a couple of throws, but Marco's desire to take us down was too fierce. Predictably, we were quickly sent to the middle.

"Okay everyone, I'm headed to the train station in a few minutes!" Jane half yelled so I could hear her at the other end of the pool.

She was going back to the city to meet her "mum," who was arriving for a two-week visit from England. "I ordered your lunch, which should arrive in half an hour."

"Thank you, Jane!" I said as I made my way to her on the deck by the shallow end of the pool. "We'll see you at home in a couple of days."

"You'll have to tell me all about the concert," she said.

When Jane told me she was going to see Harry Styles at Madison Square Garden, I immediately thought of Sam and decided to invite her and Marco to attend his concert as well. I was never into his boy band, One Direction, but I liked his solo music. More than that, I loved his genderbending sense of style; he was known for wearing sparkles and feather boas. Even though Jane had given me the idea, I'd be attending before she would.

"I don't want to spoil anything for you," I laughed. "Tell me again when you're going. A week from Saturday?"

"Yes! Should I be at your place at 7 p.m. the night you go?" she asked.

"Perfect," I said. "That's plenty of time to get to the Garden. I'm meeting Marco and Sam there, so I can leave closer to 7:15 p.m."

"I can't wait to see what you're wearing," Jane said. "Something pink and sparkly I hope!"

"Of course! Okay, you'd better get going. I don't want you to miss your train."

Once I'd nabbed our tickets, I spent an entire afternoon combing through Amazon and put together the perfect concert outfit (from head to toe): pink heart-shaped plastic sunglasses, a pink silk ribbon worn as a choker around my neck, a silver backless halter top, a pink tulle jacket trimmed in pink feathers, silver sequin bell bottoms set in a zigzag pattern, and Betsy Johnson rhinestone-studded tennis shoes.

Dressing up in sexy outfits and lingerie made me feel beautiful. It also distracted me from thinking about death and grief. There was something about putting on a costume that allowed me to step away from the constant pain and stress I'd lived with the last few years. It was a survival skill—dressing as someone else allowed me to become a woman who wasn't afraid, who still had hope for love, and who understood how strong she really was. Taking photos of myself dressed up forced me to take a shower and wash my hair. It gave me a reason to get up in the morning. I had been doing this for myself, my partners, and my Instagram account—now I was psyched I finally had somewhere to go.

I could not remember the last time I went to a concert. Steven and I had such different tastes in music, it just wasn't something we would enjoy together. Henry was very sensitive to crowds and loud noises; he even stayed in the house when Jane and I turned on the Sonos by the pool. There was no way I could have taken him to the Garden for live music.

While I was thrilled I had an opportunity to spend more time with Sam and Marco, I felt a little guilty about leaving Henry out. I wanted to believe there would be another chance for the four of us to spend time together, and then I would plan an activity we would all enjoy. For now, I really wanted to listen to live pop music.

"Mom! I'm hungry. When's the food getting here?" Henry said, leaning out of the French doors. He had gone inside to play video games and Zoom with his friends while Marco, Sam, and I hung out on the lounge chairs.

Just as I looked at my phone to check the time, a car pulled into the driveway.

"It's here," I told him. "Why don't you guys sit down at the picnic table while I go get it?"

I grabbed the large bag from the landing outside the front door and took it to the picnic table. It was late for lunch, so we all dug in, famished from hours in the pool. Marco and I chatted a little bit, but Henry and Sam didn't have much to say to each other. I hadn't assumed they would, so I wasn't disappointed, but given enough time together I hoped these two only children would become close, like I was with my brother.

On the outside, we looked like a typical suburban family of four and I imagined how much fun we would have on a family vacation. Maybe we'd spend a week in the Caribbean like I had with my mom, stepfather, and my brother, where we made so many wonderful memories together.

By the time we finished eating, Marco and Sam needed to head back to the city. I was grateful that Henry was with me. I wouldn't be left standing outside alone again, longing for someone to stay, or take me with them.

I said goodbye to Marco, but for the first time since we met six months ago, I knew when I would see him again. We had plans to meet in two days at Madison Square Garden. We had our tickets, and we knew our seats. Nothing was left in limbo.

I finally felt like my feet were planted firmly on the ground.

How could I have known the rug I was standing on would soon be pulled out from beneath me?

CHAPTER TWENTY-SIX

THE NIGHT of the concert the concourse was jam packed with teenage girls in feather boas and heart-shaped plastic glasses. We were moving in waves, ebbing and flowing, like high tide under a full moon.

I kept looking down at my phone to make sure I didn't get carried past my section. I passed concession stands selling concert "merch," coffee, and alcoholic beverages. There wasn't much in the way of food except pretzels and hot dogs. I'd forgotten Madison Square Garden was where the Knicks played their home games during basketball season. I hadn't had time for dinner, but I'd wait until Marco and Sam arrived before going back to get something to eat.

I knew I had good seats, so I shouldn't have to walk much farther . . . and then I saw it, just a glimpse of the stage and the huge marquee overhead. Finally, there was my section!

I disengaged from the gaggle of girls and entered the stadium. I was early, and there was a stillness I hadn't expected. I walked down a few steps and found my seat on the aisle.

Damn, this was awesome, and nothing was even happening yet. I turned my back to the stage and took a selfie. *Click!*

The stage was set up for an elaborate band, but the main attraction was solo singer Harry Styles. Jane and I had listened to his recent album *Harry's House* on repeat out by the pool, so I was familiar with all his new songs.

The air conditioning was on full blast in anticipation of the massive dance party that was gonna go down tonight. It was like the calm before the storm, and I was ready for all of it.

Marco and Sam arrived looking super cute in matching white feather boas.

"Amy, these seats are amazing," Marco said as Sam nodded and smiled beside him.

"We still have time before the show starts. Let's grab a bite to eat," I suggested.

Marco agreed. "Great, I'll get the drinks."

For the adults, Marco ordered the tour's signature cocktail, a themed watermelon vodka cooler named after Harry's hit single "Watermelon Sugar," while Sam got the mocktail version.

It wasn't a strong drink, but I felt lighter and pleasantly buzzed. I imagined taking Sam to another concert, but this time just the two of us. Maybe it wasn't too late for me to have a stepdaughter. How long had it been since I'd pictured anything good happening in the future? Months? Years? For me this wasn't just a fun night out—it was the beginning of new possibilities.

Back in our seats anticipation ran like an electric current through the stadium's sold-out crowd. Nineteen thousand fans were on their feet as Harry came bounding onto the stage. Showtime!

By the end of the night, we were energized and exhausted as we merged with the masses, weaving our way slowly out of the building and into the warm night air.

Marco, Sam, and I walked for several blocks before we could get a taxi back to my apartment. It was close to midnight, and we had decided that they would stay over and take the long subway ride home the next day.

When we got back to my place Henry was still awake. I was hoping he'd fallen asleep, but I wasn't surprised he waited up.

"How was the show?" Jane asked.

"Awesome," Sam replied.

"Fantastic! I can't wait to go next week!" Jane said, picking up her bag.

As I walked her to the door, Henry said, "Goodnight Jane!" He was really attached to her now, and I was grateful he had another trusted adult in his life.

"Goodnight Henry. Goodnight, all!"

I closed and locked the big metal door behind her.

Turning to Sam I said, "Let's get you set up on the daybed in my office."

After she settled in, I sat with Henry for a few minutes until he fell asleep. Marco made himself comfortable on the large couch in the living room. I went to my room, changed into my pajamas, and washed off my makeup in the bathroom before I tiptoed back down the long hallway, past the rooms where the kids were sleeping.

Marco was still awake, reading something on his phone. Everything looked so perfect on the outside. If only we could settle into our roles as . . . what? Boyfriend and girlfriend? Partners?

I longed to have him in my bed, even if we didn't have sex. To sleep next to him would be enough. I was so tired of being a widow, but I wasn't sure what came next.

I walked over to the couch, took Marco's hand, and led him to my bedroom where we undressed and got into bed. I reached for him, and he lazily responded to my touch. I couldn't help myself—I wanted him so desperately.

"It's okay babe, I'll do all the work," I whispered in his ear. "Just lay down and relax."

I straddled him, guiding him into me as I lowered myself down. I angled myself forward, rubbing the sensitive parts between my legs against his pelvic bone. As I moved to my own rhythm, he followed my lead, and I felt so close to him as we came together.

"I love you, Marco."

We'd never said this to each other before, and I certainly hadn't planned on saying it. But everything just felt so perfect. . . .

"Thank you, Amy."

I never expected him to say it back, so I had no right to be disappointed, but I was.

I tried to backpedal. "Love is easy for me. Trust is hard."

"Both are hard for me, Amy," he said.

"I know. Goodnight Marco." While it was true that I knew he had issues with love and trust, it didn't shield me from the pain of his response.

"Goodnight Amy."

Despite little sleep, we were up before the kids. Marco went back out to the couch, neither of us ready to answer questions from curious children wondering why he was coming out of my room. We said nothing about our conversation the night before, our heads cleared in the morning.

I got cereal for the kids and coffee for the adults before Marco and Sam headed home on the subway. There was no kiss goodbye, no plan set up to see each other again. Despite all we had been through, I still could not take it for granted that there would be a next time.

"Are you and Marco more than just friends?" Henry asked.

Caught off guard, I stumbled over my words before saying, "We are dating."

"Does that mean you are boyfriend and girlfriend?"

I paused before continuing, "We are dating to see if that's what we want one day, but for now, we are not."

"Okay," he said, turning back to watch a YouTube video on his computer. I was relieved my answers satisfied his curiosity.

The forecast for the day was sunny and hot. It was noon when Henry and I went back to the house in New Jersey, followed by Jane and her mum a few hours later. We still had three more days by the pool before it was time to go home for good on September first.

After a whirlwind of sightseeing around the city, Jane's mum was a little under the weather but still managed to spoil us with her cooking. The unstructured time by the pool passed quickly, and before we knew it, we were saying goodbye to summer.

Jane and her mum left after breakfast, while I stayed with Henry to make sure we left the house tidy, the way we'd found it. It was early afternoon by the time we were in an Uber on the way back into the city and I got a text from Jane:

Mum and I have tested positive for Covid.

Covid was technically "over," and we'd managed to survive without any of us getting sick, but it was still one of my biggest fears. Since Jane was positive, I couldn't rely on her help this week, which would create challenges anyway, but worse than that was my own fear of getting sick. We lived in New York City—we knew how serious Covid could be. Ever since Steven had died my biggest fear had been something happening to me—who would take care of Henry?

Henry and I didn't have any symptoms, but we still took Covid tests when we got home. Thankfully, we were both negative, and I spent the next couple of hours unpacking, doing laundry, and ordering groceries to be delivered. As I was putting dry goods away in the pantry, though, I noticed my throat beginning to feel scratchy. I took another test, and this time I sent a photo of the results to Marco.

Marco: Covid positive?

Amy: Yes. Henry is negative. I'm wearing my mask in the apartment.

Marco: Aww, I'm sorry Amy.

Amy: I just had a video visit with a physician's assistant from my doctor's office. Hydrate and rest. I don't qualify for Covid-specific meds. I feel awful, Marco. I hope this doesn't last too long. I'm scared.

Marco: I know, it shouldn't last too long.

Amy: I don't know who will watch Henry if I have to go to the hospital. Okay, my brother can always watch Henry. I hate feeling helpless. Thank you for checking on me.

Three days later, Henry tested positive for Covid, but his only symptom was a slight fever. I was relieved that I was feeling a little better every day and that a crisis was averted. Marco and

I continued to have long text conversations while Henry and I remained quarantined for another week, and he even planned to see me in person once we all tested negative!

Amy: Having Covid made me reevaluate where I want to focus my energy. I'm going to become a sex-positive influencer on Instagram, for women over fifty. I'll work on a book about what my life was like over this last year, and how I'm rebuilding it from scratch.

Matt and I had already talked about some of these ideas, but now I wanted to make them a reality. One thing that was becoming clear to me was that there were probably lots of women in a situation like mine who could benefit from my hard-won wisdom. Perhaps a small percentage of women my age were widows like me, but there were also plenty of women who had gotten divorced or were experiencing other types of loss or separation. Even women who were in solid marriages, or women who had never had children—lots of us had probably lost touch with our connection to our sexuality somewhere along the way.

I felt vulnerable sharing my plans with Marco because his support was important to me, but I wasn't sure I'd get it.

Marco: The book sounds like a great idea! Still good for me to come over tomorrow?

Amy: Yes! What time can you get here?

Marco: How about 9:30ish?

Amy: Yay! I'm looking forward to seeing your handsome face.

Marco: For that I am blessed. Looking forward to seeing yours too, Amy.

I hadn't dared to hope he missed me, but then I read how early he was coming, and that he was looking forward to seeing me too. What's more, he felt blessed that I wanted to see him so badly, and I believed him. He'd never used language like that before, which felt like a good sign—plus, he thought my book sounded like a great idea! I thought it meant that he was finally going to let me love him, and that his heart was open to falling in love with me.

I was so happy, but then I began to panic. The thought of losing him filled me with dread. If we became serious, if he loved me, then losing him would be so much harder. I wanted things to work out between us, but it was also terrifying. I wanted to run away, but I knew I had to learn to sit in my feeling of discomfort about the future. I vowed that I would be brave, intentionally keeping my heart open to him. When I felt fearful of another loss, I soothed myself with the memory of the four of us laughing in the pool. I let myself imagine the scene unfolding into a future where my family was whole again.

CHAPTER TWENTY-SEVEN

THE FOLLOWING day it dawned hot and hazy, but I kept it cool and comfortable in the apartment, the central AC humming through the HVAC system.

I buzzed Marco into the building, then took one last look at myself in the mirror. I was dressed in a new three-piece lingerie set: a clingy mesh teddy, a matching G-string, and a lace choker. The light pink color set off the glow of my sunbaked summer skin.

When I opened the door, Marco was already standing in the doorway. He flashed me the same sheepish grin as the first time we met, but we were not the same. There was history between us, and I let the possibility of new love into my heart. I felt shy and anxiously giddy under his gaze.

I needed a minute to collect my thoughts, so I asked, "Do you want some coffee?"

"Yeah, sure," he answered.

I hurried behind the large kitchen island to the coffee machine. When I turned around to hand him his mug, he was sitting on the swivel stool across from me. I stood watching as he took a sip. He was so handsome.

I couldn't stop staring at him as I thought about what a wonderful lover he was and how much I trusted him. I remembered how surprised and happy I'd been to receive his texts and photos while he was on vacation, and I was so proud of the way he and Sam finished that long bike tour.

I thought about our birthday celebration, and that Marco hadn't corrected the hotel attendant when he assumed we were married. I replayed those days we spent with our kids by the pool at the Airbnb, and the light in Henry's eyes to have a man pay attention to him again. More than that, Marco cared about me and Henry. He was there keeping me calm every day when I was so scared I might die from Covid.

Yes, I loved him. But I also loved my freedom—the freedom I only had because Steven had died. It felt easier to dream of a life with Marco and Sam when I didn't believe it was a real possibility. Now that it could be happening, my fear threatened to derail us before we even got started. So even though it wasn't the way I wanted to start our morning together, I couldn't stop myself from asking him jokingly, "So, who have you been fucking?"

Ugh. As soon as the words were out of my mouth, I wished I could take them back. I was about to apologize, tell him I was nervous, and that of course I knew he wasn't fucking anyone else when, to my great shock, he replied to my question. . . .

"I think I should end it with this current woman I'm fucking. It's just too complicated with her kid and her crazy ex-husband." He said this casually before asking, "What do you think?"

Wait. What?!

I felt a lump growing in my throat and tears pricking the corner of my eyes. All I could think was, *Do. Not. Cry.*

"Well, it doesn't really matter anyway," he continued, "because I met another woman a couple of weeks ago who lives a few blocks from me. Fucking her is very convenient, and who knows, maybe it could develop into something more. I'm not opposed to it."

I could not meet his eyes. I felt so stupid, standing there in my lingerie. How could I have thought a gorgeous man twelve years my junior wanted a relationship with me? But I had.

I wanted to die, but I told myself to breathe—in through the nose, out through the mouth. Everything was ruined, there was no salvaging it.

"Let's go out for brunch," I said, desperate to flee my apartment.

"Oh-kay," he said, obviously confused that we weren't going to fuck.

"Let's go to Café Luxembourg. It's only a few blocks from here."

I threw my clothes on while he finished his coffee, trying to use the time to steady my emotions. I wanted to appear unaffected when I came out from my bathroom.

I had no idea what to say as we walked to the restaurant, so I said nothing. I should have known it would be crowded, all the outdoor Covid tables occupied. Once we were seated inside, I immediately ordered a Lemon Drop martini.

When my drink arrived, I took a large gulp. As the vodka hit my bloodstream, I felt my jagged edges smoothing out, but inside I was dying from a thousand tiny cuts.

I felt blindsided. It was more than just the fact that he was sleeping with other women; it was that he didn't tell me until I asked. I'd shared everything about my life with him because I thought he was becoming my person. Even if that didn't mean monogamy, he was still the most important man in my life. I thought I was becoming the most important woman in his life too.

I had become adept at dissociating from my emotions but when the waiter brought our food, I felt tears prick the corners of my eyes again. I swallowed hard, finished my drink, and held it together through lunch. I didn't lean in to kiss him goodbye, but he didn't seem to notice as he smiled and said, "I hope you have a good rest of your day." I had to pick Henry up after school, and somehow, I managed not to cry until he was safely home, in my room with the door shut. I was sure Marco had no idea how hurtful he had been, men could be so dumb, although in this case it appeared I was even dumber. Emotionally exhausted, I decided to sleep on things and see how I felt in the morning.

The next day I still felt awful. I couldn't let things go, so I texted Marco to tell him that while I knew he wasn't trying to hurt me, nonetheless he did. I wanted him to apologize and to acknowledge that he should have told me about those other women sooner, preferably before he started fucking them.

Instead, it was more important for him to be right than to admit he could have handled the situation better.

Marco: I'm sorry you were hurt, but you are not going to paint me as a liar. We were friends with benefits, but you can't get over this hope for something more.

Amy: I never said you were a liar. I said you lied by omission. It never occurred to you that I would want to know who you were sleeping with?

Marco: You asked, and I told you.

Amy: I shouldn't have had to ask. I thought being in an open relationship meant being open about who we were sleeping with.

In retrospect, I realize that our expectations were vastly different, and had I not asked him who he was fucking, he never would have told me. I felt like an idiot, and I hated myself for being so stupid.

Over the next few days, we continued to text about our kids and their orthodontist appointments, as if nothing had happened. We even made plans to have dinner together the following week. I knew it would hurt to be with him under our current circumstances, but it hurt more to think I'd never see him again.

I turned all my anger inward, and my self-worth plummeted. I tormented myself with images of him with other women and created a narrative in my head that my need and my love disgusted him.

Of course I told Lisa about what had happened.

Lisa: I'm worried about you.

Amy: I'm truly unlovable.

Lisa: Not true, I love you.

But I really did feel unlovable, like there was something broken inside me. I tried so hard to mask it with the idealized images I created, but I imagined everyone could see how damaged I really was.

The only thing that got me out of bed was creating art. I sent Marco a slew of photos I'd taken of myself dressed as a naughty nurse. I was building a portfolio to post once I created my new Instagram account, the one that I'd told him about when I was sick with Covid. Essentially my idea was to build a business of some kind, perhaps as an Instagram influencer who also wrote books. Sharing my ideas about the business had made me feel vulnerable, but he thought my book idea was great. Even though I felt hurt and unlovable with him, he had always appreciated my pictures. I knew I looked amazing in these, so I felt confident posting them. But then he sent me this text:

Marco: I wonder if Instagram will throw you off for those photos.

In retrospect, I knew he didn't intend to be so hurtful, but in that moment, I saw his text as confirmation of how damaged and unworthy of love I really was.

Amy: Really? You don't like them?

Marco: Dunno.

I was crushed. I had worked so hard on those photos and been so proud of the final images. It only took two texts, a handful of Marco's words, to turn my pride into embarrassment and shame.

Regardless of Marco's feelings, I still believed others could learn from my story. I knew there were women who had lost their husbands and felt as hopeless and lost as I did, that there were women my age who were bored with their husbands, or single, or had gone through a divorce. I wanted to let them see that reinventing their lives, especially after loss, was possible.

I shut down my phone and went to take a shower. Not long ago Marco brought so much joy to my life, but now his energy threatened to destroy what little remained of my self-confidence. I turned to Matt:

Amy: I need an alias, I'm too nervous to use my real name.

Matt: What about "Jenny the Manhattan MILF"?

Amy: Why Jenny?

Matt: I don't know. Jenny sounds fun, playful. You are going to be the queen of Instagram MILFs!

Amy: Thanks babe. I appreciate your confidence in me.

I felt grateful that Matt was supportive. Even though we were no longer lovers, he continued to meet some of my emotional needs. He checked in with me every morning after I dropped Henry at school just to see how things were going. He was so excited to help me start my Instagram account, and it felt good to have someone genuinely believe in me.

As September drew to a close, Marco asked to reschedule our dinner date—he had forgotten about Sam's parent-teacher conference. I tried so hard not to become reactive and kept reminding myself about how miserable I had been the last time I told him goodbye. But my rage proved to be too much, and I exploded. I couldn't help thinking about his lie of omission and I was furious. I started a text chain that led down a bumpy road.

Amy: You hurt me! I was vulnerable and you preyed on me.

Marco: If you honestly feel that I sought to take advantage of you then I'll sever our relationship myself.

I didn't think he had necessarily taken advantage of me, certainly not maliciously, but in the moment, as vulnerable as I was feeling, I didn't know how to explain the emotions that were roiling inside.

Amy: I can't do this with you anymore. The whole time I was sick, and scared, and missing you so badly, you were with her. Are you still fucking her?

Intellectually I'd known all along that he could have been involved with other women, but I still let myself believe that he would have told me if he was sleeping with someone else. The emotions I felt for him clouded my logic, and I was overwhelmed by my neediness. I felt so angry that I couldn't help but share my feelings with him even though I knew it might drive him away. When I didn't hear back from him, I just assumed I had ruined things yet again.

My honest expression of genuine emotions should have been the end of things between us, but it wasn't for me. Losing Marco, or rather, pushing him away, triggered a grief tsunami inside me. I felt like I was drowning in a sea of pain and loneliness, desperate for someone to save me.

Steven, my husband, was dead, but Marco was alive, and I was convinced that the only way to survive was by getting him back in my life. I left him voice and text messages. I sent him long emails detailing how I would change and do better.

I held on to hope because he hadn't blocked me. When I saw that he read and listened to my messages, I was hopeful that eventually he would want to see me again. In the meantime, I felt compelled to replay our last conversation at the kitchen island over and over in my mind. His casual reveal of other women, each word stung like a slap across my face. The pain exquisite, I would then be transported to Steven's hospital room. Our last minutes together. The music, the goodbye, the oxygen machine turned off. Two final scenes fused together.

It was slowly becoming clear to me that I wasn't ready for a new relationship, and that Marco and the other men I'd been with were actually a distraction from grieving Steven's death. I realized that I was afraid that if I let myself fully feel the pain of his loss, I wouldn't be able to cope with taking care of Henry and my other responsibilities as a solo parent. But I was starting to realize that I couldn't just run away from my grief forever.

I had tried to be honest about what I wanted from men, but I was now realizing that it had probably been impossible to do this because I didn't know what I wanted from men myself. Living with my husband's incurable cancer diagnosis for three years (the last year and a half during the pandemic) caused a lot of trauma. I was grateful I already had a great therapist, but life-altering loss requires more than talk therapy to heal. I knew I needed to connect with other widows, a community that understood the confusion and isolation I was still feeling.

I was starting to realize that my way forward would be through grief rather than running away from it, and that it would take time and care to recover. I wasn't the same person I had been with Steven, so I put my energy into building my platform, paving the way for a "post-loss" version of myself.

CHAPTER TWENTY-EIGHT

WHEN I started my Instagram account in late September 2022, I still wasn't ready to accept that Marco would never speak to me again. I mourned his absence like a death, and my only respite was learning to grow on social media. In retrospect, I learned different lessons from my two types of loss. When Steven died, I ran away from my grief, believing that I could circumvent the pain by attaching myself to another man, who was flawed and messy like me. When Marco cut off all contact, I ran toward my grief, realizing that everything I needed to give myself security and comfort was within me.

I had very little experience using social media platforms in general and faced a steep learning curve as I got my account up and running. I knew I wanted to connect with like-minded people, so I searched for midlife influencers, women over fifty, and widows. A search for the hashtag #Sexpositivity led me to boudoir photographers, where I found new inspiration for my own work.

My photos were good; I was confident that they were. In the six months since I began using my tripod/ring light/Bluetooth remote combo, I'd taken at least one thousand images of myself. While I had no desire to take anyone else's picture, I thought it would be a great learning experience to book a professional boudoir shoot with a local photographer, so I jumped at the chance when I found someone with a last-minute cancellation.

Evie had a gorgeous studio in a hip new industrial complex in Brooklyn, and I paid extra to have my hair and makeup done by a professional she worked with often. She told me she shot for an hour, enough time for three to four looks, depending on how long it took the client to get comfortable in front of the camera. I had recent experience shooting closeups of my vagina, so I figured we'd be able to work quickly.

The temperature was in the mid-fifties, bright and sunny the morning of the shoot, but it felt colder since the new complex was built in a decommissioned Navy yard by the East River. After hair and makeup, Evie shot me in the four outfits I'd brought as we worked our way from one end of her mid-century modern studio to the other. We started in the bedroom area with a PG-13 look. I posed on the bed covered with black satin sheets in a black Chantelle demi bra with matching panties, a brand sold in specialty shops and department stores.

The remaining three looks I bought cheaply on Amazon: a baby blue organza bra and panty set (on a turquoise chaise), a white bodysuit with flower appliqué (on a brown velvet couch), and topless, wearing a pair of fishnet stockings with a silver rhinestone body chain (on a pink velvet seashell couch).

A week later I returned to the studio to choose twenty-five photos for my custom album, complete with a black faux snakeskin cover. I loved the images and the album when it came ten days later. Overall, the shoot had been a great experience, and I picked up some good tips for makeup, lighting, and camera angles. Of course I tagged the photographer, hair, and makeup person when I posted some of the pictures on Instagram, and it made me realize how much work I'd been doing alone.

My introduction to the online coaching industry, specifically grief groups for widows, also took place around this time, in early October. Even with the support of my own therapist I still felt very isolated in my grief. I wondered what it would feel like to talk with women who were also struggling to create new lives after their spouses died.

That was how I found a post for a widows' retreat taking place the following month—four nights in Steamboat Springs, Colorado with sixteen other widows. There was only one spot left, and something inside me knew I had to snag it.

I was both excited and scared at the thought of being away from home for so long, but once I confirmed that Jane would be able to stay with Henry, I reserved my spot. The widow leading the retreat was Emily, who had been in her early thirties when her husband died from cancer two and a half years before Steven.

She offered a few group coaching programs for widows and was about to kick off a new mentorship group for grievers who wanted to start their own businesses. I was already leaning heavily toward quitting my job at Columbia, but I wasn't sure if I could really become a full-time influencer. I had fourteen subscribers and three posts when I scheduled a thirty-minute call with Emily to discuss her new program and where I might fit in.

She immediately understood that I wanted not only to become an influencer, but also to start a movement inspiring women in midlife to love their bodies and reconnect with their sexuality. I wasn't sure I had an idea for a business, but

I welcomed the chance to work with other entrepreneurial grievers over the next six months.

I was in desperate need of a cheerleader, but also someone who understood the complexities of widowhood, loss, and grief. Through her offerings I was lifted up by a wonderful community of widows and went full steam ahead in building my Jenny brand.

Going all in gave me the strength and clarity I needed to finally quit my job. I performed a detailed cost-benefit analysis, even though I knew in my heart I could not go back. Exploring my creative work was the best way for me to move through my grief and reinvent myself. Steven had been the center of my life, but without him nothing worked anymore. I also needed the flexibility to be home with Henry if he needed me. Jane was still with us, but she wasn't a substitute for a parent when he needed one.

I emailed the Journalism School's human resources department and my boss at the Journalism School and resigned. I wanted to be completely free before I went on the widow's retreat in Colorado the following week.

I had never been to Colorado—or experienced sunshine so blindingly bright. I flew into Denver and then caught a connecting flight to Steamboat Springs. The retreat location was halfway up a mountain overlooking a gorgeous valley. There was an indoor hot tub and a private chef to cook all our meals.

It wasn't all sadness and crying, although there was some of that too. We did yoga and made a couple of trips into the little town. The highlights for me were the trip to the hot springs and the golden hour photo shoot with a professional photographer.

Everyone brought beautiful dresses and skirts, while I wore a white bodysuit covered in applique flowers. It was about forty degrees Fahrenheit, and I was barefoot in the rough grass, but the pictures were stunning, if I do say so myself.

I was glad I had prepped Henry with several hotel nights away over the previous year because he did wonderfully with Jane over the four days I was away. He only wanted to FaceTime with me the first day and when I got home, I was so proud of him. More importantly, he was proud of himself.

It was good to spend time with other widows who understood how devastating it was to lose a spouse. But while I got along with the other women, it was hard for me to form a lasting connection with anyone because my situation was a bit unique. While I was still raising a preteen, my peers (women in their fifties) all had older teenagers or college students. We were in different stages of life in terms of raising children—they were empty nesters while I was preparing myself for the dreaded teen years. The widows with kids my son's age were all ten to fifteen years younger than I was. We were in a similar stage of life in terms of raising children, but a lot happened to a woman's body between her forties and fifties because of menopause. So, I was in a unique category, sort of on my own with my particular issues. Still, I had a wonderful time and would recommend the experience to any widow seeking support and community.

Over the next few months, I continued to post on Instagram as Jenny, although I did make a video explaining that I wasn't using my real name. It became my habit to post more serious captions with lighthearted visuals, so I paired dancing in my underwear with an essay about cancer and end of life care in the hospital. The only people in my real life who knew about the account were my therapist, Lisa, and Matt.

Shortly before the end of the year, in December 2022, I posted a fun little reel I created of me dancing in different lingerie sets which I had edited together. This was the first original video I created without using a template and it was well received.

While talking with cancer widows on the retreat and online, I heard similar stories over and over about doctors not being honest with the patient and their family about the prognosis. Instead, they repeatedly pushed more aggressive treatment, which was often accompanied by harsh side effects. Many times, families felt robbed of meaningful time together at the end, and I urged readers to push for answers from a member of the hospital's palliative care team (which was not the same as hospice) because they were trained to keep patients comfortable while on treatment. Doctors were taught to treat diseases until the very end, which wasn't always what the patient and family wanted.

A friend read my essay and thought it was information more people needed to read. Up to this point I had been very rigid about my boundaries and had done a good job keeping my Jenny account separate. She thought I should cross-post on my personal Facebook account, the one Steven's family could see. I was working toward using my real name on my Instagram account while keeping my Jenny handle, and I felt the risk of outing myself was less important than my mission to help others.

I felt privileged to be alive, to have a voice, and to have access to a platform which could potentially help others, so I did it. I outed myself as Jenny the Manhattan MILF and was shocked by what happened next.

CHAPTER TWENTY-NINE

WHICH WAS—nothing. Nothing happened. I have no idea if Steven's brother, his wife, or their teenage daughter saw or read my post. I never heard anything from my mother-in-law, Steven's stepmother. My brother doesn't have any social media accounts, so I wasn't worried about him seeing anything, but I suppose somebody could have told him.

A couple of old high school friends thought it was cool and supported me, and that felt good. I was glad there were zero negative reactions, but as time went on my only real concern was for my son. I worried that one of Henry's classmates, or their parents, would see my cross-post on Facebook or find my Instagram account and he'd be bullied. But my biggest fear was that he would hate me for embarrassing him.

While all of this was happening, I was writing about it, and by this point I had an almost-complete draft of my story. I wanted to take the next steps toward publication, but my worry about Henry's future caused me to debate with myself about whether to even publish this book.

Before moving forward, I had to get really clear on my motivation for sharing this deeply personal story. I felt strongly that writing openly and honestly about my own sexual reawakening in midlife could help end the stigma surrounding female sensuality and pleasure. I wanted others struggling with feelings of shame, loneliness, and despair to see that self-reinvention and living a meaningful life were still possible after loss. I knew I couldn't control anyone else's reaction to my book, but I could show my son that I had the courage of my convictions. Ultimately, I felt it would be a disservice to us both if I gave in to my fear of what other people might think rather than be true to myself and what I believed in. I moved forward with my writing and my other creative projects.

I continued to pour every ounce of creativity I had into my photos, videos, and my captions (limited to twenty-two hundred characters, including spaces). I steadily grew my following, but an issue I seriously hadn't anticipated arose—other female midlife influencers didn't like me. I had been prepared for male haters, but the guys loved me. I wasn't thrilled that all they saw was my body, but as an older woman taking up space on the Internet, their overuse of eggplant, water droplet, and smiling face with horns emojis didn't bother me.

Most women influencers, however, wrote me off as a sex worker trying to funnel my following over to an NSFW site like OnlyFans. Many of these midlife influencers preached for women to wear whatever they wanted, regardless of age, but they saw my sensual content as catering to the male gaze and thus anti-woman.

I called a few of them out on their hypocrisy and was overjoyed when a couple of my favorites admitted they were wrong to shun me. At the same time, I began to feel solidarity with sex workers on Instagram who used their platforms to advocate and educate about the adult industry. I learned so much from these women and felt in complete alignment with their advocacy.

During my first three months on the platform, I grew my account to 130 posts and two thousand followers, but my growth slowed because I was shadow banned, which meant my content was policed on Instagram using an additional set of guidelines and wouldn't be shown to nonfollowers. Female bodies were censored, and infractions could render an entire account ineligible for recommendation to anyone but current followers. As my account stopped growing, I began advocating for sex workers' rights, including decriminalization and destigmatization of all forms of sex work.

I questioned the narrative that sex work was inherently dirty and dangerous rather than a byproduct of a criminalized system. Stigmatization was driven by the history of a puritanical culture and moralistic ideology. I saw bipartisan laws created to suppress sex workers under the false guise of protecting children from sex trafficking and pornography.

In practice those laws restricted First Amendment rights for all Americans by threatening social media companies with millions of dollars in fines for web hosting any content which might have been construed as prostitution. This disproportionately affected women and other marginalized groups who risked being deplatformed and losing all their content and followers.

No one seemed to care because these social media bans were primarily affecting sex workers, who were always the test cases for any new restrictive legislation. Once a precedent was set, it became easier to enact more restrictive laws and implement higher fines affecting mainstream audiences. This made me even more determined to share my images and my story.

I took matters into my own hands in February 2023, the second Valentine's Day since Steven's death, and sent myself two dozen long-stemmed red roses, free-trade artisanal chocolates, and a rose-patterned demi bra with matching thong made by Fleur du Mal Lingerie (on the higher end, but not over the top La Perla). I set up everything in my bathroom and created a rose-themed "behind the scenes" video which I voiced over:

To celebrate Valentine's Day, I thought I'd give you a little behind the scenes look at one of my photoshoots. You can see my tripod and ring light in the mirror, which I'll adjust so you can't see it in the background when I'm filming. I've already done my hair and makeup, so now I'll do a few poses while I record. I used slow motion on the part where I fanned my hair, so it looks super sexy. I have fun playing around with the mirror, so you get a good view of the back. And that's it, pretty simple!

A month later I created a backup Instagram account, @jenny.takes.manhattan, in case Meta deactivated my main account. Backups were standard for "spicy" content creators, which included anything related to women's bodies, sex, or sexual pleasure, even in an educational context.

By that time, I had ten thousand followers, and I knew a few lingerie models, boudoir photographers, and sex workers who'd had their accounts shut down without warning, losing all their followers and content in the process. "Spicy" included women in bikinis, women pole dancing, women in lingerie, etc., but explicit pornographic content was forbidden on both Facebook and Instagram, a policy I supported and agreed with.

However, the lines were sometimes blurry. I assumed Meta removed a photo of me wearing a sexy maid's costume because I took it at the Mandarin Hotel, and I stupidly tagged them. I figured they must have reported me for a Content Guideline violation because I had spicier images that were not taken down.

At the end of May 2023, I started an OnlyFans account using my backup handle, @jenny.takes.manhattan. It took me a while to get into the mindset to start on that platform, but once I did, I wondered what had taken me so long. I had a lot of male Instagram followers who asked me if I had an account, or whether I would consider starting one, although that was not a deciding factor.

Ultimately, I made that move because I was tired of not being paid for my hard work. My Instagram followers liked my content and wanted to pay for it, but I was barely allowed to post any of my work, let alone earn any money from it. I was angry that Meta would not allow me to monetize on their platforms because I showed some skin. It was demeaning to have my body policed, but when men made crude comments, they suffered zero consequences. The double standard was infuriating and reinforced a culture where "boys will be boys" but women were slut-shamed.

I was also curious to see how much money I could make on a platform devoid of sexist and puritanical restrictions. I was lucky to be financially secure and not dependent on that income to pay my rent and living expenses, unlike the influencers I knew on Instagram who really struggled to pay their bills when their accounts were shut down. On the flip side, many OnlyFans influencers risked losing their earning potential if they refused to post progressively intimate content which subscribers often demanded. I too felt the pressure to reveal more, but I could quit whenever I wanted.

I set my subscription price at $9.99 per month for all content posted to my feed. I soon learned that the real money was in pay per view offers that were DMed to subscribers at regular intervals. This was where the more "hardcore" content came into play. I didn't find it difficult to create short clips of me taking a shower or doing a striptease, but developing posting schedules for pay per view content became a chore. I didn't want to make the same offers over and over, but I didn't want to miss an opportunity to offer older content to new subscribers.

That meant segmenting subscriber lists by date and tracking offers, which sucked all the fun out of having the account in the first place. My subscribers also wanted content that was raunchier and rawer, which meant less creativity on my part. They didn't care about lighting and makeup and the little stories that I liked to make up.

Anyone could masturbate with a vibrator while fucking a veiny Caucasian dildo suctioned to the wall (including me, as it turned out), but I also wanted to create sensual images in five-star hotel rooms with Central Park views. I was interested in creating art, but no one wanted to pay for that. Males made up 90 percent of my following on both platforms, but I hoped to attract more female followers on Instagram, especially widows and grievers.

It wasn't easy because many women were put off by my content because they were uncomfortable with their own sensuality and sexuality. I challenged them to put my images in the context of a woman who was grieving the death of her husband, but women turned out to be much more judgmental of a woman embracing her body than men were.

I found their judgement of me was rooted in cultural, religious, and patriarchal narratives created to control women's bodies and keep them financially dependent on men. I urged women to become curious about the source of any internalized misogyny and to question who benefited from conflating their worth and societal status with their "purity" and virginity. The oft used excuse "that's just the way it is" was devoid of critical thinking, and thus for me, was a nonanswer.

Overall, OnlyFans was not a horrible experience, and I appreciated the opportunity to monetize my work. But I didn't like being pressured to create more explicit images. Also, some of my male subscribers felt that paying for my content entitled them to ask for whatever they wanted, including my time. I was constantly stressed about keeping up with my DMs (which I had already disabled on Instagram).

Unfortunately, I was sidelined when the boots I bought a month earlier to wear in a sexy cowgirl photoshoot (seven-inch rose gold platforms) caused my lower back pain to become unbearable. An MRI showed a herniated disc was compressing a couple of nerve roots, so I chose to have microdiscectomy surgery two days before my fifty-sixth birthday at the end of July 2023. I was in and out of the hospital the same day, but I took a month-long break from posting content while I healed.

Luckily, I made a full recovery, but I was shaken by the surgery experience. I realized how alone I really was, and I felt a reawakening anger at Steven. I'd spent three years taking care of him, or watching Henry while he received treatment, and now, I had no one to take care of me. Six weeks after surgery

I was cleared to begin physical therapy, and I started going three times per week. I felt weak, fragile, and scared I might hurt myself irreparably unless I got serious about maintaining muscle mass and strengthening my body. I continued physical therapy for a year and started doing the exercises at home when my health insurance wouldn't pay for it anymore.

I decided not to continue on OnlyFans after my surgery. The pressure to post more explicit content and the fear of reinjuring myself led me to deactivate my account, even though I had risen to the top 2.6 percent of creators. After six weeks on the platform, I chose to prioritize my physical and mental health rather than continue to measure my worth by an arbitrary ranking and how much money I could earn.

CHAPTER THIRTY

IN SEPTEMBER 2023 I celebrated my first year on Instagram. I felt so proud of the content I had consistently created (more than three hundred posts), and the twelve thousand following I built. Even though it had been a year since I last saw Marco, and all my attempts to contact him had gone unanswered, I still left him a message about my surgery. I thought if he had truly ever cared about me, he might have a kind word, but no. I guess I really didn't think he would respond, but I was still disappointed when he didn't. I wish I could say this changed my behavior and I never contacted him again, but I sent him a short text or photo of me and Henry a few more times. He never responded, but I still wished him and Sam well.

I made it through my first year of widowhood by looking for a man I could rely on, even though I didn't necessarily realize I was doing that at the time. While this was certainly an understandable approach, it was ultimately not successful—all it did was cut me off from my emotions and my own sense of power. But I made it through my second year of widowhood with the creative outlet my Jenny the Manhattan MILF account provided. It allowed me to explore the parts of myself I'd kept suppressed for so long and connect with a community that made me feel seen and supported. That was empowering, authentic—and all me.

It was a good thing my priority was not making money because I literally earned pennies through Instagram's bonus program for digital creators. In fact, I actually paid Meta to boost some headshots (acceptable content) because that was the only way I could get posts in front of nonfollowers. I set a budget for my boosted content under advertising, but despite using the platform's spending limit tools, I paid thousands of dollars growing my following to fifteen thousand. Still, I was proud that for the first time in my life I bet on myself, and I discovered I was worth it.

I continued creating new content and taught myself various video editing software. I even began to make music video-esque content where I would lip sync and act out the song lyrics while dressed in lingerie or a costume.

Most of these videos were under ninety seconds, but my epic masterpiece (ha ha) was set to Queen's "The Show Must Go On." It began with me wearing a sweatshirt and folding laundry in my bedroom and transitioned to me wearing a Greek goddess costume searching through the ruins in ancient Rome.

Throughout most of the video I wore the skimpy maid's costume while I did chores around my apartment: baking cookies, sweeping floors, doing laundry, emptying the dishwasher, and making the bed. I used many video editing techniques such as swapping out backgrounds, changing replay speeds, and using special filters. This song with my video was a visual representation of how I felt at the time as a solo parent doing all the things while grieving and exhausted. I had so much fun creating this video, and I was thrilled that my widow and grief community loved it.

I also created a few original video shorts, including a take-off on *The Real Housewives of New York* called *The Real Widows of New York*. I made three one-minute episodes starring me as Amy Gabrielle, Jenny, and the host Andrea Cohen. They were silly but allowed me to show off some of my video editing and script writing skills.

Throughout my first year on Instagram, I continued to occasionally treat myself to a night in a hotel room in the city while Jane stayed over with Henry. I always went alone. After everything that happened with Marco, I didn't want to meet any other men in person. I wasn't completely off dating apps, but I just chatted with men occasionally when I felt lonely.

I tried several different five-star hotels throughout Manhattan and a couple in Brooklyn. I always brought my photoshoot equipment, two or three new costumes or lingerie sets, and a pair of platform heels. Everything fit in my rolling carry-on luggage, so I felt like I had a secret, like I was on a secret mission.

When Steven died, I thought I needed a new man to move forward with my life and feel happiness again, but now I focused on pleasing myself and doing what brought me joy. This included things like my photoshoots, which usually took about an hour from start to finish, including hair and makeup. I never scouted locations ahead of time, I just took multiple photos and some video from different angles. I usually had great views, so there were many images taken in front of windows at sunset or sunrise. On clear nights I got great shots with the New York skyline as a backdrop.

In November 2023 I was extremely lucky to have the opportunity to study with a creative visionary and one of my favorite influencers. Known on Instagram as Lux ATL, she founded "Stripcraft, a playground of sensual movement and sexy travel providing good times for bad girls worldwide since 2014!" She was also a former university professor who was offering a six-session virtual writing course using her real name, Dr. Lindsay Byron.

Dr. Byron was hands down the best writing instructor I ever had. She used prompts to get us writing immediately and by the end of the course I had three polished works. When she offered the course for a year beginning in February 2024, I jumped at the chance to work with her again for such an extended period.

Two weeks later I started my own Substack at Dr. Byron's suggestion and began publishing some of the assignments I wrote for class. I knew I wanted to write about my life as a widow the year after Steven died. I couldn't find any other widow stories even remotely like mine. I thought that was probably because of the stigma women feel about all things sexual.

Surely there must be others who were grieving in a way like I was, but I couldn't find them. I thought my story might not only help normalize the topic of sex after one's partner died but also help women in midlife who were reinventing their lives after becoming empty nesters or going through a divorce. I felt I had a unique perspective to bring to the discussion midlife women were having about self-reinvention, and I felt called to contribute my voice.

I started to spend more time writing and connecting with other writers on Substack and less time doing photoshoots and posting on Instagram. I felt less inspired shooting videos and photographs in sexy outfits, while growing creatively as a writer. I still do the occasional shoot when I want to reconnect with my body and sensuality, but for the past five months, from August through December 2024, I've been using the sex organ between my ears much more than the one between my legs.

As I continued to write and do the work of considering life after widowhood, I thought more about who I had been in my past long-term relationships, and a clear pattern began to emerge. I had repeatedly toned down my personality and my sexuality because I didn't think a man would love me unless I made myself smaller, attracting less attention. Steven's death deconstructed my life in ways I never could have imagined. I was shocked to realize how much of myself I had suppressed when I met him.

He'd offered safety, security, and predictability, and that's what I wanted. He never asked me to change, but somehow, I felt that I had to. It was interesting to notice how much of myself I had been suppressing throughout my life. I wondered why I acted this way repeatedly and looked back to events from my childhood to see how they affected my social-emotional development.

I was five years old when my mother divorced my father in 1972; that's when my personality split in two. I had a good relationship with each of my parents, but never at the same time. Depending on how I lived my life from year to year, I was either the wayward daughter or beloved child. I learned at an early age that if I wanted to be loved, I had to close off parts of myself because no one was going to accept all of me.

I had always been my mother's closest confidant, and she raised me to be a women's rights activist, to appreciate the benefits of travel, the flexibility of part-time or temporary work, and spending money on life experiences over material things. My father was cautious and craved stability and predictability. He had a government job in accounting and a pension at retirement. He didn't approve of my mother's life, or most of mine, but when I got married at forty, he was ecstatic. I was finally in a steady relationship, and I had a full-time job and a 401(k) plan again. The only other time in my life we had been that close, I was in my mid-twenties getting my master's in arts administration. We bonded over the accounting courses I took alongside MBA students. On the flip side, my mother felt betrayed and basically cut me out of her life. She only wanted a surface relationship with me, the extent of which was the occasional holiday dinner with my brother's family.

Had Marco and I gotten together, I was sure I would have sacrificed parts of myself to be with him and make our relationship work, the same way I always had. This time I would have been motivated by my fear of raising my son alone while grieving Steven's death. I didn't think I was strong enough to do either of those things on my own, but over this past year I had discovered that I was wrong about this. Marco was gorgeous, and we had great sex, but at the end of the day I wanted the freedom to fully express myself without fear of judgment.

Eventually, my focus turned to writing, and my platform of choice was Substack. That's when I came to the realization that to move forward with my memoir, I had to separate myself from Matt. Telling my story required an honesty we couldn't share, and I would have wanted his approval before I published anything.

Again, I would have shut down parts of myself to please a man, but this time I wouldn't even get his love in return. I decided to delete my Snapchat account, which was the main way we communicated. It wasn't easy to cut Matt out of my life; he had really been a source of support and encouragement. In retrospect, I could have handled our break-up in better ways than just deleting my Snapchat account, but I wouldn't have been able to write this memoir otherwise.

Facing the last two years head on, without a man, or men, to distract me, has been the most painful experience of my life. But I chose to go through it. I chose not to dissociate again or chase my feelings away with men and sex.

Grief began to feel more like a mild to moderate chronic condition rather than an acute, yet curable, disease. Mourning Steven's death became a part of who I am. Sometimes I still have grief-fueled flare-ups, other times I don't have any symptoms at all. Ultimately, I had to redefine what happily ever after looked like for me.

In my twenties and thirties, I was more susceptible to societal messages about what I should want to be happy. Number one on the list for women was, and still is, a man's love. From Disney movies to stupid lines like, "You complete me," we are meant to believe getting a man to love us is really all we need to be happy.

After we get the man, we are supposed to want babies. Women get sidetracked running a household and/or working outside the home while men are allowed to pour themselves into their careers. When women try to do that, we are met with mom-shaming and guilt. It is a fine line to walk, and we usually find ourselves on either side of it, rather than squarely on it, feeling like we're failing at both.

By midlife many women have all the things that are supposed to make us happy, but many of us are not. I don't know if "happily ever after" was ever a realistic goal, but at this point in my life I value peace over happiness. My life became chaotic when Steven died, everything changed, and I had to find my place in the world again. It took me three and a half years to get back to myself and to begin living a more authentic life.

My midlife friends are also thinking about what they want for the second half of their lives. Some are mourning the death of a parent, the loss of a job, or their child-centered lives as their kids become young adults. Grief can be a catalyst for growth as we understand on a much deeper level that our time on Earth is not unlimited.

Many lists have been compiled of the top five regrets of the dying, and a version of the following is often number one, "I wish I'd had the courage to live a life true to myself and not the life others expected of me."

So, take it from me: If you haven't been living your life as your authentic self, now is the perfect time to start.

EPILOGUE

December 2024

THROUGHOUT the writing of my memoir, I felt scared that my story would end on a sad note, which was the opposite of what I wanted. After my relationship with Marco ended this fear intensified. How could the ending be happy and uplifting if I wasn't in a relationship? Then it dawned on me that my happy ending was about having a peaceful life, living as the truest version of myself, and focusing on my desires without seeking permission or approval from anyone else. At the end of the day, happiness had nothing to do with whether I was in a relationship or not.

A couple of days ago I saw my therapist for the last time in 2024. The next time we would see each other it would be 2025 and I would have gotten through the fourth Christmas and New Year's Eve without Steven. I felt a little anxious knowing I wasn't going to see her for two weeks, but she always said I could call her cell in an emergency.

At 9:15 a.m., I opened Zoom and saw her familiar smile. To me she looked just like a blonde Julia Roberts.

"Hi Amy!" she said with her usual enthusiasm.

"Hello!"

I never quite matched her sunny temperament, but some days were better than others, and that was a good day.

"Is there something specific you want to talk about today, Amy? How are you feeling going into the Christmas break?"

"I'm feeling pretty good going into the break, but there is something I wanted to talk about, something that's shifted for me recently." I paused for a few seconds to collect my thoughts. "I've started to remember how I felt about Steven the first couple of years we were together. I guess I always remembered how much I loved him, but I had forgotten how it felt. Does that make sense?"

I had started seeing my current therapist shortly after Steven was diagnosed with incurable cancer in August 2018, so she never knew pre-grief Amy. By the time we met I was already so angry with him for not taking care of himself. I rarely allowed myself to feel the deep love we shared before cancer blew up our lives. Of course, my therapist knew I loved him, but when we met, that love had already been permanently stained by grief.

"Yes, of course that makes sense. Cognitively, we might know we had a specific feeling, but unprocessed trauma kept us from feeling it in our body."

"I feel like I just woke up from a dream. It's the same happiness I felt when we got married in 2008, but I also feel sad because he's not here. I miss him," I said, feeling my voice break. I was trying to describe the overwhelming feelings of love I could now access, the love I remembered as if it had just happened yesterday.

"Traumatic loss can change our perception of time," she said, using her most compassionate tone.

It was close to the end of the session, so I blew my nose and wiped my eyes. I didn't mind ugly crying during our meetings, but I liked to end them feeling grounded.

"It's strange to feel opposite emotions from different periods in time simultaneously, but it makes sense. Grief isn't linear," I agreed.

We ended the session by wishing each other a peaceful new year before logging off.

Afterward, I sat for a few minutes reflecting on my experiences over the last three and a half years. There was much heartbreak, but also tremendous growth through creativity. I felt proud of the goals I had set and my determination to accomplish them—I built a successful social media platform, I wrote a memoir, and I rebuilt a peaceful life that is true to who I am now. I celebrated the moment by taking a picture of myself (fully clothed), sitting at my dining room table, where I did most of my writing. I needed an updated headshot to accompany my author bio, and that felt like the perfect time and place to capture the new me.

ACKNOWLEDGMENTS

THIS BOOK could not have been written without the support and enthusiasm of many people. Thank you Brooke Warner and the Stable Book Group for taking a chance on me. Thank you to the talented team at She Writes Press, especially my project manager, Megan Milton, for keeping me on schedule, Lindsey Cleworth, for my gorgeous cover design, Anne Durette, for copyediting, Julia Denardo Roney, for proofreading, and Lindsey Salatka, for additional editing. So much gratitude for my publicity team at Mindbuck Media: Jessie Glenn, Rae Aniskevich, Bryn Kristi, Kari Olson and Deborah Jayne. Thank you for holding me together when I felt like I was falling apart.

A huge thank you to my amazing developmental editor and cheerleader Kathleen Furin. There would be no book without you asking me how each scene made me feel. Thank you Lindsay Byron, PhD (aka Lux ATL), a true artist and gifted writing teacher and my Weekend Writers group for jump-starting my writing after many years. Thank you Emily McDowell and the 100DayProject group for welcoming me so warmly and building my confidence as I wrote my first draft. To Jessica Buchanan, thank you for your early support before I had a clue about what I wanted to write. Thank you Clover Stroud for leading a truly transformational memoir writing retreat at your lovely home Washington, DC. It was an honor to learn from the best!

Thank you to Elizabeth Gilbert, Margaret, and all the "lovelets" writing Letters From Love on Substack. This is truly an amazing community, and I am especially grateful to Mesa Fama, Bonnie Solomon, and Kaylen Alexandra who championed my writing from the beginning. Thank you Brendan Spiegel from Narratively who did a wonderful developmental edit for me early on. Thank you to my widow sisters and grief coaches on Instagram, especially Emily Bingham and Mira Simone. Thank you to all the spicy content creators leading the way to decriminalize and destigmatize sex work, especially Pomma and Mistress Mei. I'm grateful for the midlife writers and influencers who embraced me, Skylar Liberty Rose, Paulina Porizkova, and Jennifer Pastiloff.

I have so much love and appreciation for Charlotte Davey and her sidekick, Milo. Thank you Valerie Walsh Valdes and Aaron Ring for your early feedback and over thirty years of friendship. Thank you Dr. Nicole Ives for fifty-plus years of sisterhood, and to my brother, thank you for your dark humor–it's always a pleasure doing business with you. To my amazing son Henry—your hard work and perseverance inspire me to keep going when life feels hard. You will always be my sunshine, and I am so proud of the young man you are becoming.

ABOUT THE AUTHOR

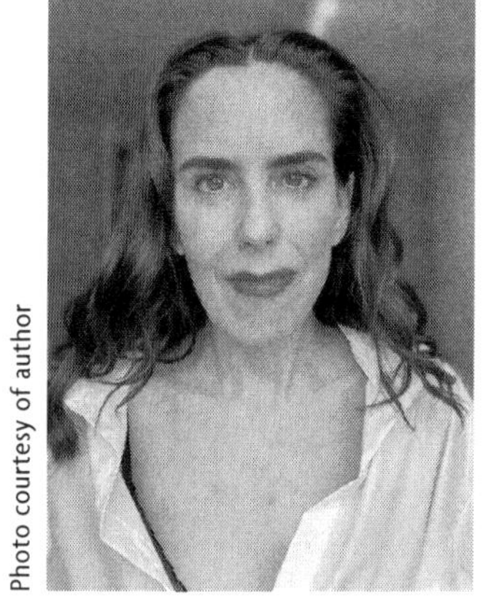

Photo courtesy of author

AMY GABRIELLE is a writer, digital creator, and advocate for authentic self-expression in midlife women. Following her husband's death from cancer, she began using memoir and social media to explore the complex intersection of grief and desire, cultivating a community of thousands drawn to honest conversations about life after loss. Her work appears in *Absolute Pleasure* on Substack, as well as Medium publications including *The Memoirist* and *Slackjaw*. She lives in New York City, where she enjoys photography, travel, and raising her son.

Looking for your next great read?

We can help!

Visit www.shewritespress.com/next-read or scan the QR code below for a list of our recommended titles.

She Writes Press is an award-winning independent publishing company founded to serve women writers everywhere.